SACRAMENTO

Pro Football's FIRST Triathlon City

Gary Cobb

Foreword by: Greg Tranter

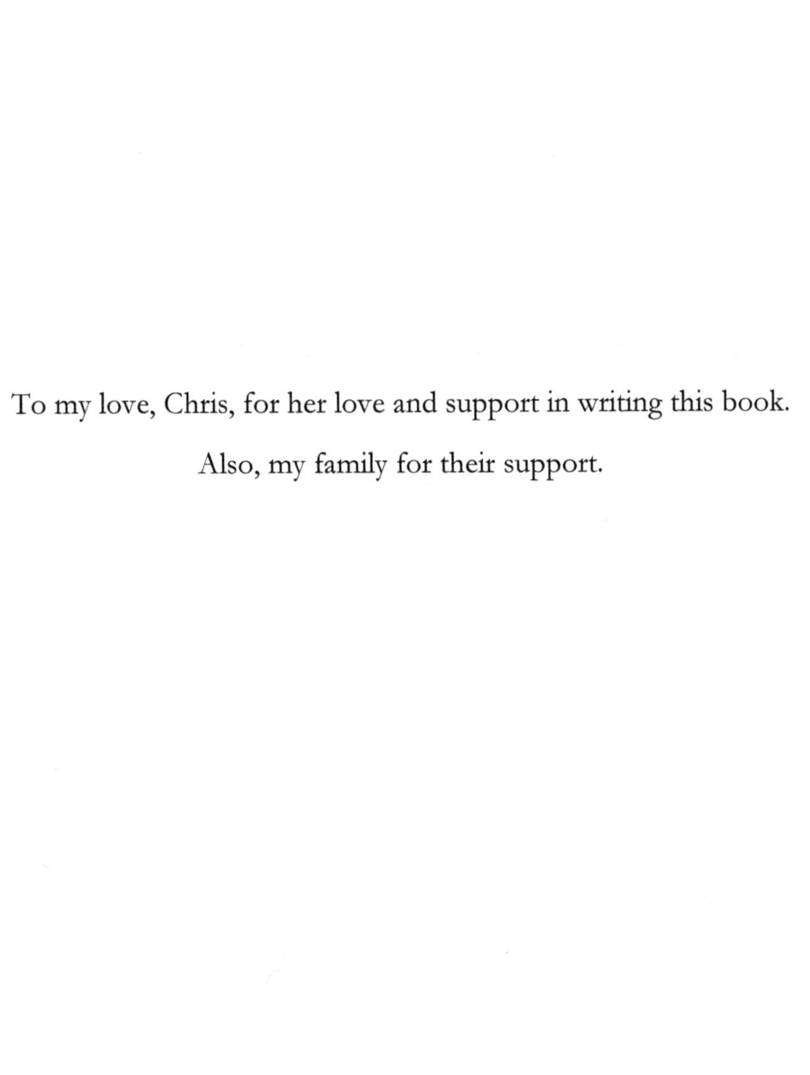

To my love, Chris, for her love and support in writing this book.

Also, my family for their support.

Table of Contents

Foreword

This is a little-known story in professional football history and even among historians of the city of Sacramento. In this well-researched book, Gary makes interesting and unique connections across Sacramento's three professional football teams of the early 1990s in the city's up-and-down history on the pro gridiron.

Sacramento is not well known for its pro football history. It has never had a team in the National Football League. It has shown up in the last half-century with franchises in several fledgling pro football leagues that did not survive. The city even tried a stint in the Canadian Football League, but that did not last either. The city's only major professional sports team in its history is the NBA's Sacramento Kings, which have played in the city since 1985 and are still seeking their first league championship in California. The franchise was a member at the founding of the National Basketball League (that later became the NBA) in 1945 as the Rochester (New York) Royals and won the league's first championship. After stops in Cincinnati and Kansas City, the franchise found its way to Sacramento.

The city of Sacramento is most well-known for the California Gold Rush, which began in 1848. Gold-seekers poured through the city in search of riches, and gold mining is still a recreational activity today. Sacramento was incorporated as a city in 1850 and became the permanent California state capitol four years later. The confluence of the American and Sacramento Rivers led to its economic success. It was the western terminus of the Pony Express in 1860 and 61 and was an important city in the development of the Transcontinental Railroad, which began construction in 1863. Today, Sacramento is the sixth largest city in California, the fourth largest metropolitan area in the state with a population of 2,680,831 (2020 census) and the 26th largest in the United States.

Sacramento's first foray into professional football was in the Pacific Coast Football League (PCFL) in 1946 and 47. The PCFL was a professional minor league that began play in 1940 and lasted until 1948 with teams primarily from California. Sacramento's team was nicknamed the Nuggets (paying tribute to the Gold Rush). It lasted only two seasons while winning only two games. Professional football returned to the city in 1964, and for two seasons, the Lancers represented Sacramento in the Northern California Football League, finishing with 7-3 and 5-5 records, respectively. In 1967, the city had a franchise in the Continental Football League that had begun play in 1965 and was a highly respected minor league with many players going on to have NFL careers. Sacramento, known as the Buccaneers in 1967, finished with a 2-10 record. The team changed its name to the Capitols in 1968 and played two more seasons before going out of business at the end of the 1969 season. In their final season, the team finished in second place in the Pacific Division but lost in the first pro football playoff game in Sacramento history, 31-0, to the Las Vegas Cowboys.

The city waited 22 years before another professional football team would call Sacramento home. Then, three different teams in three different leagues came to Sacramento between 1991 and 1993. This book picks up the story from there, analyzing each of these three fledgling franchises and the hope and excitement they brought to the capital city. Gary offers some interesting perspectives and insights into a period when these three grid teams called Sacramento home in a five-year period when football was the talk of the town. Since those teams left, pro football has only returned once for a brief stint in the United Football League from 2009 to 2012.

Gary has uncovered a unique pro football achievement that no other city can claim. He calls it the Pro Football Triathlon. In this book, he brings this interesting and unique story to life.

Gary is a renowned Arena football expert, founder of the Arena Football League museum and a pro football historian. He provides a compelling narrative with Sacramento's ins and outs in the pro game while providing many unknown records set and firsts in pro football history.

Join Gary as he walks down this distinctive path in Sacramento history that very few, except maybe the most ardent Sacramento sports fans, may know.

Sacramento

On a chilly November night inside Hughes Stadium in Sacramento, California, a crowd of 9,444 fans watched the Continental Football League playoff game between the hometown Capitols and the visiting Las Vegas Cowboys. This game was played on Saturday, November 29, 1969, and was a forced playoff game due to the fact that both teams were tied for the Pacific division at 8-4-0. Not only were their records tied, but in the head-to-head games, they were tied, each winning two games and losing two games, with the Capitols winning the last two 31-10 and 13-10 with both played in Sacramento. Each team was going in different directions coming into the game, as Las Vegas was on a four-game losing streak, while Sacramento had a four-game winning streak. The winner of this game was to face the San Antonio Toros for the Western Conference Title.

After a scoreless first quarter, Las Vegas scored on a nine-yard Bob Humphery field goal, then added a two-yard run by HB Bobby Burnett, making the score 10-0. As the half drew close, the Cowboys added another score as LCB Marv Pettaway returned his interception 80 yards, giving the visitors a 17-0 halftime lead. Hoping to rebound in the second half, the Capitols were attempting a 47-yard FG when it failed, and Pettaway returned the missed kick 92 yards for another touchdown, giving Vegas a 24-0 lead.

In the final quarter, the Cowboys added another score, a three-yard run by RB Mike Vogel, making the score 31-0, putting the game out of reach and ending the Capitol's hopes of a championship. The following morning's paper read, "Cowboys Wallop Caps in Playoff 31-0." With wallop being the keyword, Sacramento was outplayed, gaining only 169 total yards with only eight first downs and being held without a point!! What the over 9,000 fans at the game never knew was that they had just witnessed the last pro football game in the city of Sacramento for years to come.

The city of Sacramento is the capital city of the state of California, and with a population of 2,397,382 people, it is the fifth largest metropolitan area in California (according to the 2020 census). The city was founded in 1850 and is the home to California's Supreme Court and the major center for all of the state's healthcare industry, with Sutter Health, UC Davis School of Medicine, and UC Davis Medical Center, to name a few. Sacramento is also home to many of the state's museums, with Crocker Art Museum, California State Railroad Museum, The California Museum (Hall of Fame), the Old Sacramento State Historic Park, and Sacramento International Airport. The city also has many nicknames, such as City of Trees, River City, and Camellia City, and is also called "America's Most Diverse City."

Sacramento, like many cities in the United States, enjoyed the game of football, yet it wasn't until 1967 that the Continental Football League (or CoFL for short) granted the city its first professional football team. So the Sacramento Buccaneers were born and played their first game on Saturday, August 26, 1967, against the Eugene Bombers. The game was played at Hughes Stadium in Sacramento in front of 10,006 fans who watched as their team defeated the Bombers 26-20. Then the Buccaneers lost their next three games by a combined score of 114-23, losing to the Seattle Rangers 23-16, then scoring just seven points in a 50-7 defeat to the Orange County Ramblers, next losing 41-0 to San Jose Apaches. Finally, on Sunday, October 1, at home, the Buccaneers got their second and final win of the season, a 24-10 victory over the Victoria Tyees.

Also, if losing games was not enough, the players threatened to quit after not receiving any game checks for the last two games. Team owners and players would reach an agreement, which stated as such: The players agreed to a $75.00 per game pay cut but would get more say in the team affairs. Adding to the problems was that head coach Don McCormick suddenly quit along with four of his assistants. The owner hired former Oakland Raiders player Joe Barbee as an interim head coach. McCormick finished 2-5-0, while Barbee would go 0-5-0, as the Buccaneers would cancel three of their last five games. Two of these games were against the Long Beach Admirals and one against the Eugene Bombers. Sacramento would go on to lose their final five games by a combined score of 165-27 as their offense scored 10 points in just one game, a 48-10 loss in their final game of the season. In their 12 games, the Buccaneers managed to win only two games, being outscored 366-110 and scoring 10 points or more only four times (two of which were the two wins). The financially troubled team was sold in March of 1968, as the Sacramento Professional Sports, who were 70,000 dollars in debt, sold the team to Lee Baldarelli, who then changed the name to Sacramento Capitols in honor of the city being the state capital. The team hired a new coach, George Porter, who had coached Monterey Peninsula College in 1961 to the Coast Conference Title with a 6-3-0 record.

The 1968 season saw the Capitols finish at 5-7-0 with a much-improved offense, scoring less than 10 points once this season, a 14-6 loss to the Las Vegas Cowboys. The Capitols scored 218 points while allowing only 248 points, which was a 118-point difference from the 1967 season. Sacramento finished in third place, winning their final game of the season 27-6 over the Spokane Shockers.

In their third season, 1969, the Sacramento team had their best season to date, finishing at 8-4-0 and tied for first place in their division. The team's offense scored just 192 points, while the defense was vastly improved, allowing only 162 points, an 85-point difference from the '68 season and a 203 difference from the '67 season. Despite the fact that the defense had improved greatly, in the playoff game against Las Vegas, both the offense and defense fell flat, as mentioned earlier. Following the loss, the owners planned to return for the 1970 season when a series of events caused the team to fold. First, the future of the CoFL was in doubt, forcing the team to try and sell 3,000 season tickets to stay afloat, of which they only sold half, around 1,500, which made the playoff loss their last game as the team folded.

After three seasons and two owners, two different nicknames, three coaches, one playoff game, one winning season (their last), and a 15-21-0 record with just one four-game win streak, which was at the end of the 1969 season, the pro football era in the city was now over. It would be another 21 years before pro football was to return to Sacramento.

While there was no pro team in Sacramento after the Capitols folded in 1970, the Arena Football League did have two games in Sacramento during their barnstorming tour of 1989. These games were held at the Arco Arena, with the first taking place on July 22, 1989, which featured the Pittsburgh Gladiators facing the Chicago Bruisers, which was attended by 7,182 fans. The odd thing about this game was that even though the game was close and high-scoring, it was the fight roughly four minutes into the game, which most fans will remember. The fight started when a late hit was not called, which resulted in both benches being emptied onto the field, and it took ten minutes for them to break up. While the officials were deciding who to eject, Pittsburgh's coach, Joe Haering, ran onto the field to object that Chicago's QB Ben Bennett was not being ejected for his part in the fight. League President Jim Foster overruled the officials, stating they could not throw Bennett out. This got Joe Haering mad, which then caused him to punch Foster in the face. When both teams saw Foster and Haering fighting, it caused both benches to clear for a second time. When everything finally got settled and the game resumed, Pittsburgh defeated Chicago 47-38. After the game, one fan was quoted saying that at first, he was not sure if he was watching a football game or a hockey game, but when things got under control, the game was fun to watch. (My thought on this game is that it was kind of funny the game was between the Gladiators and the Bruisers, as both teams' nicknames refer to fighting)

Coach Haering was suspended for two games for hitting Foster. The next game was the Arena League's playoff game, with the Gladiators facing the Denver Dynamite at the Arco Arena with 5,417 fans in attendance. This game did not have any fighting, but it was a great game with the Gladiators trailing 37-32 with 23 seconds left when Pittsburgh's QB Willie Trotten found WR Brian Gardner with a 30-yard touchdown. Then Pittsburgh's defense sealed the victory when Linebacker JoJo Heath picked off Denver's Mike Rhodes pass, giving the Gladiators a 39-37 win. The following week in the Arena Bowl, the Gladiators would be defeated by the Detroit Drive 39-26.

After the Arena playoff game, pro football was gone again in Sacramento until the summer of 1990, when the World League of American Football (WLAF) would come to town.

WLAF 1991

On a rainy, soggy March evening inside Hughes Stadium, a crowd of over 15,000 witnessed the first game of the World League of American Football in Sacramento. After a 31-year hiatus, pro football was back in the River City. This game was between the visiting Raleigh-Durham Skyhawks and the home team called the Sacramento Surge. Trailing 3-0 in the final quarter, Surge head coach Kay Stephenson pulled struggling QB Ben Bennett in favor of QB Mike Elkins. (Bennett, you might remember, played for the Chicago Bruisers in the Arena league game played back in 1989 at Sacramento's Arco Arena. The game was most remembered for the fight that cleared both benches.)

Surge's Mike Elkins quickly led his team to the game's first and only touchdown. A one-yard run by Running back Paul Fraizer, but the two-point pass failed. Next, Elkins drove his team to their final points, a 28-yard field goal by Kendall Trainor, who had missed two earlier tries from 38 and 34 yards.

The rainy conditions helped produce a combined nine turnovers and a total of only 382 combined yards. A downpour during halftime drove most of the crowd away, leaving only several hundred fans to see the victory.

The World League of American Football, or WLAF for short, was born in March 1989 as the NFL owners agreed to fund the spring league. The original plan for the WLAF was to have 12 teams, with four in Europe, one in Canada, one in Mexico City, and six in the US, with play to begin in March of 1991. Sacramento was the sixth city to receive a franchise when, on June 8, 1990, - the WLAF awarded the River City a team. Sacramento was the farthest western city in the league, with San Antonio being their closest rival, roughly 1,735 miles away. Even though the city had a team, it had no owner and no stadium (the league awarded most cities a franchise even before there was an owner). Next, on November 19, 1990, it was announced that Fred Anderson would be the majority owner of the club. Anderson was the founder of Pacific Coast Building Products Inc. (a company that supplied building supplies throughout the western states) and was a major investor with the Sacramento Sports Assc. which helped build the Arco Arena . Anderson went to work with naming the team, which was to be called the "SURGE" after the surging Sacramento River. Then he named former NFL and Buffalo Bills head coach Kay Stephenson as the first coach in the team's history. Stephenson had coached the Bills from 1983 to 1985 with a 10-26- 0 record before being fired after four games in 1985. Finally, Anderson set up an agreement with Hughes Stadium for the 1991 season. With the start of the first season just four months away, league officials were still pushing for the 12-team league, but by December 20, they settled for a 10-team league without a team in Italy or Mexico City. The league then awarded the final team to the joint cities of Raleigh-Durham. The WLAF divisions were as follows: the European division had the London Monarchs, the Barcelona Dragons, and the Frankfurt Galaxy. In the North American East were the Montreal Machine, the New York/New Jersey Knights, the Orlando Thunder, and the Raleigh-Durham Skyhawks. In the North American West were the Birmingham Fire, the San Antonio Riders, along with Sacramento.

Finally, on the weekend of March 21 and 22, the WLAF kicked off their first season with games in London, Orlando, Barcelona, San Antonio, and Sacramento. As mentioned before, the Surge hosted and defeated Raleigh-Durham 9-3 in their opener. In Week Two, the Surge headed to Birmingham for a divisional matchup against the Fire inside the legendary Legion Field. With the game tied at 10 and the Surge driving for the go-ahead score, QB Elkins dropped back to pass when Birmingham LB John Miller intercepted his pass and returned it 99 yards for the winning score.

Sacramento had a chance to tie the game in the final minutes, only to fail after having a first and goal at the Fire two-yard line. Sacramento would lose 17-10, with 16,432 fans in attendance.

In Week Three, the Surge was on the road for their divisional game against the Riders in San Antonio. In this game, the Surge led at halftime 3-0 before the Riders scored 10 points in three minutes to take control of the game. The Surge again had a chance to take the lead when QB Elkins fumbled the snap, which led to a Riders 31-yard field goal that ended the scoring. Sacramento would lose 10-3, failing to score even a touchdown. The Surge was now 1-2-0 and had lost two divisional games. There were only 6,772 fans that attended this game.

In Week Four, the Surge would play host to Frankfurt in a game for the record books as a crowd of 17,065 fans filled Hughes Stadium to witness this historic event. What was so special about this game? First, the Surge scored more than 10 points for the first time all season. Second, the Surge managed to record the first win over a team from Europe as they defeated the Galaxy 16-10. This win came after eight other tries. Frankfurt opened the scoring when Galaxy running back, Tony Baker, scored from three yards out. Next, Sacramento returned a fumble 66 yards for a touchdown, but the extra point was blocked. Then, the Surge added to their lead when QB Elkins threw a 33-yard pass to Carl Parker. The Surge scored the only points of the second quarter as Mike Trainor kicked a 46-yard field goal. Sacramento went into the halftime leading 16-7. Both teams played through a scoreless third quarter, with the Galaxy adding the only points, not only of the last quarter but of the half. Frankfurt drove to the Surge's 31-yard line in the closing seconds before the drive failed, with Mike Perez's final two passes falling incomplete, giving the Surge a hard-fought win and a spot in the history books.

Up next was a Monday night prime-time game against the New York/ New Jersey Knights played at Giants Stadium. Sacramento scored 17 first-half points, including a Kendall Trainor 25-yard field goal with 5:19 left in the half. The Knights opened the scoring as quarterback Jeff Graham took the ball in on a six-yard run. The Surge scored the next 14 points both on two Elkins passes, the first a 19-yard pass completion to Derek Holloway and then a 13-yard strike to Carl Parker. The Surge led 14-7 after the first quarter, yet the lead was short-lived as Knights RB, Eric Wilkerson, scored from nine yards away, tying the game at 14. Trainor added his 25-yard kick, giving the Surge the lead. Then, with just 25 seconds left in the half QB Graham scored again on a one-yard run, giving the Knights the lead for good, 21-17. Each team scored once in the second half, making the final score 28-20 in favor of the Knights. A good crowd of 21,230 were in attendance.

For their Week Six game, Sacramento had a nice crowd of 19,045 to watch the Surge play the Dragons. Once again, this game would place both teams in the record books for the first overtime game in the brief history of the league. With the Surge trailing 20–6 in the final quarter, Sacramento QB Elkins led two scoring drives; the first was a six-yard pass to WR Parker, the next was a six-yard run by RB Leon Perry, and a successful two-point pass to Parker tied the game at 20, forcing overtime. Barcelona got the ball in overtime and drove to a 36-yard field goal by K Massimo Manca.

As the Surge began their drive (Remember, in the WLAF, both teams would have a chance to get the ball in overtime before it became sudden death. A field goal does not win the game unless each team touched the ball.), QB Mike Elkins released the ball only to have it intercepted by Barcelona linebacker Eric Naposki, who returned it 27 yards for the winning touchdown as the Dragons won 29–20.

The Surge entered Week Seven with a 2-4-0 record, and the Montreal Machine was coming to town. For Sacramento, the good news was that Montreal was 2-4-0 as well. Both teams played through a scoreless first quarter, then, just 30 seconds into the second quarter, the Surge scored with K John Nies nailing a 31-yard field goal. As the quarter wore down, a total of 23 points were scored, and the Surge was leading 13–10. Once again, the teams played through a scoreless third quarter. The fourth quarter started with the Surge scoring on an 18-yard pass from QB Elkins to WR Parker. On the ensuing kickoff, Montreal scored as Richard Shelton returned the kick 90 yards, helping Montreal stay in the game. (earlier in the game, Shelton had returned a punt 67 yards for a score).

Montreal scored again when QB Mike Proctor ran in from 14 yards out. The Surge responded and tied the game at 23 when Nies kicked a 31-yard field goal with six seconds left on the clock. The extra quarter almost went the full 15 minutes, but with three seconds left, Machine kicker Bjorn Nittmo kicked a 30-yard game-winning field goal, giving Montreal an exciting 26–23 win. With the loss, the Surge lost their second straight overtime game as 17,326 fans witnessed the game.

Week Eight would see Sacramento enter the record books yet again as they traveled to Orlando to play the Thunder. Orlando scored the first 14 points, first on a 43-yard run only 3:09 into the game and then on a seven-yard pass. The Surge scored on a Paul Fraizer one-yard run to cut the lead. By halftime, Orlando was leading 21–19 as their special teams blocked two of Sacramento's extra points. As the second half started, it was the Thunder's special teams that scored on a 20-yard blocked punt return. Then, it was their defense that scored on a seven-yard fumble return. By the end of the game, the Thunder outscored Sacramento 45–33 in a game that saw 47 first downs, 313 total rushing yards, and 496 yards in passing. Both teams combined to score 78 total points, setting a WLAF record with 20,048 fans watching.

By the time London came to town for a Week Nine matchup, the two teams were headed in different directions, with the Monarchs still undefeated at 8-0-0 and the Surge were 2-6-0 and out of the playoffs. Sacramento could play the role of spoiler with a win over London. As fate would have it, things did not go the Surge's way. By the time Sacramento scored with four seconds left in the half, London had scored 31 points, led 31-7, and coasted to a 45-21 victory. Sacramento made the record books again, this time by playing before the FIRST sellout crowd in league history as 21,409 packed Hughes Stadium, a small crowd for a sellout, yet a sellout nonetheless.

Sacramento traveled to Germany to play their final game of the season against the Frankfurt Galaxy. To get to this game, the Surge had to travel 5,617 miles and 11 hours and 44 minutes (a long way to go to play just one game of football). Frankfurt was still alive in the playoff hunt, and a win would help them out greatly, while the Surge was looking to finish a disappointing season. Sacramento could play the role of spoiler by defeating the Galaxy. After playing through a scoreless first quarter (again), the Surge opened the scoring as Elkins connected with Parker for a six-yard touchdown.

Frankfurt countered the Sacramento score as Perez threw a 20-yard strike to WR Craig Morton. After the half, Running back Tony Baker scored on a two-yard run for the Galaxy, giving them a 13–7 lead as the extra point was missed. The Surge shutdown Frankfurt as Sacramento scored the next 17 points en route to a 24-13 upset of the Galaxy, damaging their postseason hopes. Frankfurt now needed the Monarchs to beat the Dragons to make the playoffs, and their hopes would be dashed as Barcelona defeated London 20-17 in an upset as well. The Surge's defense forced three Galaxy fumbles, recovering two of them, making four interceptions of Perez, and sacking him three times. This victory for the Surge made them the only North American team to win in Europe. The largest crowd (51,653) in WLAF history was on hand to witness this upset. (another record for Sacramento).

Here are some of the highlights and records from the Sacramento Surge's first season:

- Won their inaugural game vs Raleigh-Durham– 9–3
- First North American team to defeat one of the European teams- 16–10 over Frankfurt - (Week 4)
- First overtime game… (Week 6)..... against Barcelona 29—Sacramento 20
- First sellout crowd….21,406 — (Week 9) against London…a 45–21 loss
- First North American team to win in Europe, (Week 10) a 24-13 win over Frankfurt
- Largest crowd to attend a game …51,653 fans at Frankfurt in a 24-13 win
- Most miles traveled to play a Official Football game 5,617 miles from Sacramento to Frankfurt 11 hours and 44 minutes—(see below)
- Most combined points scored; both teams (78) Week 8…..(Orlando 45–Sacramento 33)

The Surge also played in the second overtime game in Week Seven, against Montreal in a 26–23 loss.

WORLD FOOTBALL TRAVEL NOTES:

1) New York Stars to Honolulu (WFL) 4,956 miles, 10 hours and 45 minutes
2) Philadelphia Bell to Honolulu (WFL) 4,908 miles, 9 hours and 30 minutes

3) Jacksonville Sharks to Honolulu (WFL) 4,654 miles, 8 hours and 31 minutes

4) Orlando (Flor) Blazers to Honolulu (WFL) 4,757 miles, 9 hours and 30 minutes

5) Charlotte Hornets to Honolulu (WFL) 4,922 miles, 10 hours and 15 minutes

6) Boston Patriots to San Diego (AFL4) 2,989 miles, 6 hours and 31 minutes (these were listed to show that Sacramento's trip to Frankfurt was the most miles traveled to play one "official" game of football).

WLAF 1992

The 1992 WLAF season started with changes both on and off the field. To start with, the team owners were not sure if there was to be a 1992 season until October of 1991, which is when the NFL owners voted to have another season. One major reason was that the NFL owners had just signed a new three-year television package with both ABC and the USA networks. Then, there was the need to replace Raleigh-Durham. The Skyhawks folded after their 0-10-0 season in 1991. The Ohio Glory was added to replace them. The Glory hired former Miami Dolphins guard and Hall of Famer Larry Little as the head coach and would play their games in Columbus, Ohio. The next change was one that was new to both the league and pro football in general, as the league added this rule that all 10 teams would play their final preseason game, and it would count in the league standings. This game would count as a tiebreaker if needed to determine playoff participants right after head-to-head competition. This rule could also help with playoff sites.

In the Sacramento Surge's final preseason game, newly added quarterback Dave Archer played a great game, going 14 of 24 for 116 yards, with one touchdown and one interception as he helped the Surge defeat Montreal 21–14.

Archer had spent eight seasons in the NFL, four with the Atlanta Falcons, after originally being drafted by the Denver Gold of the original United States Football League (USFL). Archer chose to sign with Atlanta as a free agent, and after four seasons with the Falcons and with little results, Archer left, spending the next four seasons with three other NFL teams: Washington 1989, San Diego 1989, and Philadelphia 1991. So, after eight years in the NFL playing for four different teams, Archer decided he needed a change, so he signed with the Surge.

Surge. Week One vs Birmingham (March 21)

Now, with all the pieces in place, the Surge began the 1992 season at home against the Fire with 17,143 fans in attendance inside Sacramento's new Hornet Field. David Archer had a great game, going 18 of 23 for 272 yards with two touchdowns and one interception. Archer seemed to move the ball at will, leading the Surge to a 20-6 victory over Birmingham, with the offense generating 360 total yards while the Sacramento defense allowed only two field goals and just 249 total yards. This would be the second straight home opener and season-opening victory for the Surge. They had defeated the Skyhawks 9-3 in 1991. But this season was to be special for both the Surge and the city of Sacramento. Why is this?

As the 1992 season unfolded, each game the Surge played would be another game in the record books, whether they won or lost. Over the course of the next year, the City of Sacramento would become the pro football's first triathlon city! But you ask, "What is a Pro Football Triathlon?" Well…Websters defines a triathlon as an endurance multisport race consisting of three events (swimming, cycling, and running over various distances). So then, what is a football triathlon? In the case of the city of Sacramento, they had three pro football teams playing three different styles of football in three different pro leagues over a period of one year! So, let's take a look at this amazing feat!!

We already saw how the Surge started the '92 season, So let's go on to week two.

Week Two in Ohio (March 29)

Heading into week two, the Surge had to travel to Columbus, Ohio, to play the league's newest team, the Glory, inside Ohio Stadium…home to the Ohio State Buckeyes, with 37,837 fans in attendance. The Glory grabbed the early 6-0 lead on a yard run by Amir Rasul, but the extra point failed. Then the Surge went to work as Archer found wide receiver Eddie Brown for a 48-yard touchdown strike. Then safety Louis Riddick broke through the Glory line, hitting Ohio Quarterback Babe Lafenburg and causing him to fumble. Surge defensive end George Berthume picked up the loose ball and scored from one yard out. Next, kicker John Nies connected on a field goal from 48 yards away, setting a team record and giving Sacramento a 17-6 win. Archer had another solid game, completing 18 of 34 passes for 160 yards with one touchdown and no interceptions.

Week Three vs Montreal (April 4)

In their week three battle with Montreal, the Surge would score first as Archer tossed a 16-yard pass to wide receiver Stefon Adams to give the Surge a 7-0 lead early in the second quarter after a scoreless first quarter. The lead held up going into the half and through a scoreless third quarter. Montreal finally scored to tie the game three minutes into the final quarter after being held scoreless through three quarters. The Surge responded by scoring on their final drive of the game, with just over two minutes left to secure the victory 14–7.

There were two key plays on that final drive that led to Sacramento's victory. Wide receiver Carl Parker broke free of the coverage to make a diving catch of Archer's pass deep in Montreal territory. Two plays later, running back Mike Pringle scored from one yard out. The Machine got the ball back and drove to the Surge's 23-yard line, but Sacramento linebacker Mike Sinclair sacked Machine quarterback Anthony Dilweg to end the game. The home crowd of 21,024 went home happy. Another highlight of the game was the Surge defense as they rose to the task, recording five sacks while holding Montreal scoreless for three quarters. Now at 3-0-0, for the first time in team history, the Surge would face a division rival.

Week Four vs San Antonio (April 11)

Coming into this game, Sacramento knew it would be a rough game against division rival San Antonio. The Surge jumped out to an early 13-0 lead. As the first half wound down, the Riders scored a touchdown with only 10 seconds remaining to cut the Surge lead to 13-7. The game was scoreless in the third quarter, but early in the final quarter, Riders kicker Jim Gallery booted a short kick, making the score 13–10. Sacramento then moved the ball down the field again, and this time, it ended with Pringle's eight-yard touchdown run. Sacramento now led 20-10 with nine minutes to play. The Riders got the ball back and marched down the field, using up over six minutes on the clock. The drive ended with running back Ivory Lee Brown scoring from one yard out. Now the Surge were clinging to a three-point lead with just over two minutes left in the game.

San Antonio's defense forced Sacramento to punt. Then their offense moved down the field to the Surge 20-yard line, setting up kicker Jim Gallery's kick to tie the game as time ran out.

In overtime, San Antonio got the ball first and moved to the Surge 36-yard line before Sacramento's defense forced the Riders to attempt a 36-yard field goal. Gallery converted his third field goal of the game, and San Antonio led 23–20. Sacramento reached their own 35-yard line but faced a fourth and 15. Archer completed a 38-yard strike to wide receiver Eddie Brown to San Antonio's 27. However, Brown was stripped of the ball, and the Riders recovered, securing the overtime victory. A crowd of 20,625 fans were on hand for this exciting game.

Week Five at Birmingham (April 18)

Sacramento traveled to Birmingham to play the Fire in a rematch of the week one game, which the Surge won 20-6. This game was to be the first stop on an 18-day journey covering 12,341 total miles for Sacramento. The Surge was positioned to take the lead early in the fourth quarter as they drove to the Fire 18-yard line. But on the next play, Archer threw a pass that Fire linebacker Paul McGowan stepped in front of for an interception.

Birmingham then scored on a 56-yard pass from quarterback Brent Pesse to wide receiver Willie Britton for the go-ahead touchdown. Later in the quarter, with Archer leading a drive to tie the game, a Surge fumble ended any hopes of Sacramento winning. A few plays later, the Fire scored on a one-yard run by running back Jim Bell to make the score 28-14, and Birmingham went onto a much-needed win with 20,794 fans on hand.

Week Six at London (April 26)

The next stop on Sacramento's 18-day road trip was London, England. There were 18,653 fans in attendance to watch this game between the Monarchs and the Surge. London would open the scoring as former Miami Hurricane running back Leonard Conley ran in from seven yards out. Three minutes later, Sacramento tied the game as Archer hit Eddie Brown with a 26-yard touchdown pass. Archer would add two more touchdown passes before the end of the first half. First, he hit wide receiver Carl Parker with a 31-yard touchdown strike and then a Hail Mary pass of 45 yards to Parker to give the Surge a 21-10 halftime lead. London scored 17 second-half points, yet it was not enough as Archer connected with Parker for his third score of the game, and Archer's fourth touchdown pass of the game was a career-high. Sacramento won the game 31-26, making the record books once again as the first North American team to win in London. The Surge was now 4-2-0 on the season and heading to Canada for their final game of the 18-day trip.

Week Seven at Montreal (May 5)

This game was the final game of the three-game road trip with the Surge playing against the Machine. The last time these two teams met, the Surge won in a defensive battle 14-7. Montreal opened the scoring with a Bjorn Nittmo 44-yard field goal, and then the Surge countered with a 20-yard touchdown pass from Archer to wide receiver Stefon Adams. The Machine scored a touchdown to regain the lead early in the second quarter, 10-7. Archer then went to work tossing a pair of touchdown passes. The first was a seven-yarder to tight end Paul Green, and then he threw a nine-yard strike to Brown. With those two scores, the Surge took control of the game 21-10 just before the first half ended. Montreal came out in the second half trying to regain control of the game as they ran nine minutes off the clock. The drive ended with a Mike Proctor two-yard pass to Adam Bob. A successful two-point conversion cut the Surge lead to only three points, 21-18.

Sacramento needed only 62 seconds to regain control. Archer threw his fourth touchdown pass of the game, an 80-yard bomb to the speedy Brown, and the Surge was back in the lead by 10, 28-18. After the Machine added a field goal, Archer threw his fifth touchdown pass of the game, a 23-yard toss to wide receiver Mark Stock that sealed a 35-21 win for Sacramento.

Archer tied a league record with five touchdowns in a game, and he also completed 23 of 37 passes for 368 yards and no interceptions. The Surge defense hounded Proctor all day, recording seven sacks for 47 yards in losses and snared two interceptions. It was a nice way to end an 18-day road trip. There were 21,183 fans in attendance.

Week Eight vs Frankfurt (May 9)

Sacramento finally returned home to host the Galaxy with a crowd of 22,720 fans on hand. The two were headed in different directions, with the Galaxy at a disappointing 2-5-0, while the Surge was 5-2-0 and fighting to make the playoffs.

The game was no contest from the start as Archer connected with his favorite target Eddie Brown, on a 58-yard touchdown pass, and the Surge never looked back as Sacramento dominated Frankfurt 51-7. The Galaxy's only score came on an electrifying 107-yard interception return by linebacker Antony Brady. The return was a league record. Archer went 22-34 for 350 yards and three touchdowns. Each of the three touchdown passes went to Brown, the star receiver, who finished the game with five receptions for 148 yards. Surge running back Mike Pringle added two touchdowns and 113 yards rushing. Yet the game ball went to the Surge's defense as they held Frankfurt to just five first downs with four sacks, two interceptions and just 65 total yards allowed (a league record).

This was the third time in two years that the Surge defeated Frankfurt, the only team to do so. The 51 points scored by the Surge was the most points scored by a single team all season and the second most in the two-year history of the league. (Orlando set the record in 1991 by scoring 58 points against Raleigh-Durham) This game ranks sixth all-time in most points by one team in league history.

Week Nine vs Ohio (May 15)

In their final home game of the 1992 regular season the Surge hosted the Glory with 21,272 fans in the stands. The Surge were in a tight division race with San Antonio and Birmingham increasing the importance of this contest. This was the second meeting between these two teams. Sacramento won the first one 17-6 in Ohio. The teams played through a scoreless first quarter before David Archer connected with Parker for a 45 yard touchdown. Archer later threw a 59 yard touchdown pass to Brown to end the half with the Surge in command, 14-0. In the third quarter the two teams played through another scoreless quarter. In the final quarter Archer found Brown once more, this time for a 74 yard touchdown. With the Surge leading 21-0 Ohio coach Larry Little replaced quarterback Babe Laufenberg with Greg Frey. He then led the Glory to their only score when he connected with wide receiver Walter Wilson for a 18 yard touchdown, making the final score 21-7. It was the Surge's fourth straight win. Archer threw for over 300 (320) for the third straight game. (368-Montreal, 350- Frankfurt) Once more the Surge defense keyed the victory as they sacked both Ohio quarterbacks nine times for 76 yards in losses. They kept Laufenberg under wraps throughout the game as he completed only 5-13 passes for just 37 yards with one interception. The Surge now stood with a 7-2 record and a chance to win their division with a win in their last regular season game.

Week Ten in San Antonio (May 23)

The final week of the 1992 regular season saw the Surge in San Antonio to play the Riders with the playoffs and the Division title at stake. In front of a crowd of 19,273, San Antonio scored first as Ivory Lee Brown ran in from seven yards, but the point after failed, and the Riders led 6-0. As the second quarter got underway, so did Surge running back Doug Debose. He scored twice in the period. The first came on a 15-yard run just 53 seconds into the quarter. His next score was a two-yard jaunt that gave Sacramento a 14-6 lead. San Antonio, sensing their playoff hopes fading, staged their comeback as quarterback Mike Johnson threw two touchdown passes to give the Riders a 21- 14 halftime lead. His first was a two-yard flip to tight end Ronnie Williams. He then tossed a short pass to wide receiver Darrell Colbert for a two-point conversion to tie the score 14-14. Johnson's second touchdown pass went to tight end Danta Whitaker from six yards away, giving the Riders the halftime lead. After the break, Sacramento's defense took control of the game. They allowed the Riders only 50 total yards of offense in the second half. The Surge's defensive play allowed their offense to score 13 unanswered points. Archer threw a 17-yard pass to Eddie Brown and Cary Blanchard kicked two field goals, one from 28 yards and the other from 19 yards, as Sacramento defeated the Riders 27-21 enroute to their first and only division title and a spot in the postseason. Archer threw for 315 yards for the fourth time in as many weeks. Brown became the first wide receiver in league history to gain over 1,000 yards in one season, and he had nine touchdowns in the last five games. Both players helped the Surge to an 8-2-0 record and the division title. Archer also had a 107.0 quarterback rating.

Playoff Game vs Barcelona (May 31)

The playoff game versus Barcelona was the first one in 23 years for the city of Sacramento. The Dragons were a better team than their record showed, and they were eager to avenge their World Bowl loss to London last season.

The Surge came into the game having scored the second-most points in the league and allowed the third-fewest. Barcelona had scored the fewest points in the two-year history of the league with only 104 points in ten games, but they were a playoff team.

The game started slowly, as the teams fought through a scoreless first quarter. The Surge scored first as safety Louis Riddick returned an interception 12 yards for the score. Sacramento was the only team all season to not return an interception for a touchdown until now. Barcelona countered with a 35-yard field goal by Teddie Gracia just seconds before the end of the first half.

To begin the second half, the Dragons got the ball but failed to advance it. On the ensuing punt, Surge returner Eddie Brown scored a touchdown on an electrifying 86-yard return. (Brown had never returned a punt for a touchdown). The Surge now led 14-3. Barcelona's quarterback, Scott Erney, went to work throwing for two touchdowns. The first was a 90-yard bomb to Dempsey Norman, but the two-point pass attempt failed. Four minutes later, Erney connected with tight end Dmetrius Davis for the go-ahead touchdown, yet again, the two-point run failed, to give the Dragons a precarious point lead of 15-14. As the teams entered the final quarter, the Surge put together their best drive of the game, moving to the Dragons' 44-yard line. The drive ended there, and Blanchard kicked the game-winning 46-yard field goal. The Dragons tried to mount a comeback but could not move past their own 45-yard line. Erney's final two passes fell incomplete as the Surge held on for a hard-fought 17-15 victory.

The Surge was outplayed as Archer completed only 9-26 for 76 yards with one interception. Brown, the league's top receiver, was held without a catch. The Surge's offense had only 15 yards of total offense in the first half and only processed the ball for eight minutes and 27 seconds. Barcelona held the ball for over 40 minutes for the game, while their defense held the Surge to just one third down conversion in 10 tries and held Sacramento runners to 21 total yards rushing. Yet when it counted, the Surge's defense once again rose to the task, stopping the Dragons when it mattered the most.

Championship teams find a way to win when they don't play their best, and that's exactly what the Surge did in this game! There were 23,640 fans in attendance to watch what would be the last WLAF playoff game in Sacramento.

WORLD BOWL 1992 at Montreal (June 6)

World Bowl II was played at Montreal's Olympic Stadium, with 43,789 fans in attendance to see the Orlando Thunder and Sacramento Surge compete for the championship of the WLAF. Both teams finished at 8-2-0 in the regular season, while they each won their playoff game, with the Thunder winning easily 45-7, over Birmingham. Orlando was a seven-point favorite to win the championship.

The Thunder scored first when quarterback Scott Mitchell threw a 10-yard pass to wide receiver Chris Ford. This touchdown was the only point of the first quarter and capped a 12-play, 98-yard drive.

The Surge then got on the board when Blanchard kicked a 32-yard field goal that ended a 14-play, 56-yard drive, cutting the Orlando lead to 7-3 in the second quarter. Orlando scored the next 10 points with Mitchell throwing an eight-yard touchdown pass to wide receiver Willie Davis, and then Tracey Bennett kicked a 20-yard field goal, and the Thunder appeared in command with a 17-3 lead. The field goal was set up by Malcolm Frank's interception of Archer at midfield, and then Frank returned it to the Surge nine-yard line. Three plays later, Bennett kicked his field goal, and things were looking bleak for Sacramento.

With just 54 seconds left before the half, Archer led a six-play, 72-yard drive that ended with Blanchard's 24-yard kick that cut Orlando's lead to 11 points, 17-6, and gave the Surge a little momentum.

The teams battled through a scoreless third quarter. Finally, early in the final quarter, the Surge offense came to life. Archer led a 10-play, 85-yard march that ended when he threw a 12-yard touchdown pass to Paul Green in the back of the end zone. Archer then completed the two-point pass to Mark Stock.

Now trailing 17-14, the Surge defense turned up the heat. First, they stopped a good Thunder drive when they forced Mitchell to fumble, and the Surge recovered. Unable to reach the end zone, the Surge attempted a field goal, but it failed. Orlando then tried a time-consuming drive, hoping to drain the clock, but a Surge pass rush forced Mitchell into a bad pass that was intercepted by linebacker Mike Jones. He returned it to Orlando's 34-yard line. Archer then worked his magic as he completed a 31-yard pass to Mike Pringle. Three plays later, Archer concluded the drive with a two-yard touchdown pass to Eddie Brown. Blanchard added the extra point, and the Surge led for the first time in this game, 21-17.

Sacramento's defense controlled the remainder of the game, never giving Orlando any chance to score. When the gun sounded, Sacramento was the World Bowl Champion. They became the first and ONLY North American team to play in and win the World Bowl. Archer was named the game's MVP as he completed 22-33 passes for 286 yards with two touchdowns and one interception.

Sacramento Records and Highlights:

- Only North American team to beat the Monarchs in London. (31–26)
- Only North American team to win the World Bowl.
- Played in the only World Bowl in North America, which was also the last WLAF game played in North America.

- Had the first wide receiver (Eddie Brown) to gain over 1,000 yards receiving, finishing with 1,011 Yards and 12 touchdowns.
- David Archer had six games of 300 plus passing yards and a quarterback rating of 107.0 as he completed 194 of 314 passes for 2,964 yards with 23 touchdowns and seven interceptions.
- Their 51 points in one game rates sixth all-time. (1) Scotland 62 (2003), (2) Orlando 58 (1991), (3) Barcelona 55 (2001), (4) Frankfurt 54 (2002), (5) Rhein 53 (2000), (6) Sacramento 51 (1992)
- The Surge defense had 39 sacks on the season, with linebacker Mike Sinclair leading the team with 10 sacks, while future wrestler Bill Goldberg had three sacks.
- Future investment guru Pete Najarian played linebacker for the Surge in 1992, and former Rams defensive star and Pro Football Hall of Famer Jack Youngblood was in charge of special projects.

The Sacramento Attack

Even before the Surge had finished the first stage of this historic Triathlon, the second stage was already underway as the Sacramento Attack of the Arena Football League were already into week two. The fact that the Attack were even in their second week was based on a lot of hard work and determination! Let's see how a bunch of events had to happen just to get the team to play in 1992.

Following the 1991 season, the Denver Dynamite franchise was sold to Jim Hartman, a Denver entrepreneur, who in turn moved the team to Los Angeles, renaming them the Wings during a press meeting on March 6th,1992. Hartman then named former CFL/NFL quarterback Joe Kapp as the team's first head coach.

Kapp, as of 1992 was the last quarterback to lead California University to their last Rose Bowl appearance in 1958. He also led the British Columbia Lions to their first Grey Cup victory in 1964. Kapp led the Minnesota Vikings to their first division title and postseason appearance in 1968, followed by their first Super Bowl appearance in 1969 when they lost to the Kansas City Chiefs.

Within days of announcing the team's nickname, Hartman and the League were served with a legal notice ordering that Hartman change his team's name or they would be sued. The Wings nickname was already copyrighted by the Los Angeles Cycling Club of the National Cycling League for the past two years.

On April 16th, 1992, League President Joe O'Hara stated that the league took action to avoid any legal battle as he states;" The league gave you (Hartman) until 5 p.m. pst on March 31,1992 to take action concerning the team name or the league would take action." O'Hara goes on to say that the nickname "Attack" was chosen as the new name, with navy blue and old gold as the team colors. O'Hara stated that the nickname was a given based on the pending lawsuit. The lawsuit and O'Hara renaming the team made Hartman unhappy, and he just walked away from his team, forcing the league to oversee the team.

Then, on May 7,1992 O'Hara announced that the franchise was moving to Sacramento, keeping the nickname and colors as well as their head coach Kapp. The Attack would play their home games at the Arco Arena, which was built by Sacramento Sports Association and was owned by former Surge Owner Fred Anderson which gave him a small part in this team as well.

The Arena League worked out a deal with the Arco Arena and the NBA Kings, which was that the Arco Arena would operate the Attack with the right to buy the team at the end of the season.

Game One (at Dallas)

Finally, it was time to play some football as the Attack headed to Dallas to face the Texans in front of 5,034 fans .(this was average attendance for an arena game). Dallas opened the scoring on a 29 yard field goal by David Chapman. Sacramento countered with a 37 yard touchdown pass from quarterback Mike Hold to wr/db Wayne Coffey. Dallas would score again as their young quarterback named Todd Hammell was just beginning his Arena career. Hammell threw a 30 yard touchdown pass to wr/db.

Tyrone Thurman giving the Texans a 10-7 lead, but the Attack would score the next 10 points to take a 17-10 lead after the first quarter. First, the Attack added a 46 yard field goal by Kevin Greene, while OL/DL lineman Niu Sale returned his interception seven yards for a touchdown. In the second quarter, Sacramento was outscored 8-3 as Dallas recorded a safety, and Thurman returned a missed field goal try 56 yards for his second touchdown of the game.

Attack kicker Greene added his second field goal of the game, a 40 yarder giving the Attack a 20-18 halftime lead. As both kickers missed a combined five extra points.

As the second half got started, so did the Texans as their defense hampered Sacramento's offense, and quarterback Mike Hold allowing the Attack to score only seven points the entire half which came, when Dallas' Thurman fumbled in his own end zone and the Attack's Pat Gregory recovered for the score. Meanwhile, the Texans scored five touchdowns to take a 49-27 win, as Dallas also forced four Sacramento turnovers.

Game Two (Orlando)

In week two, the Attack was hosting the Predators in the newly opened Arco Arena. Orlando scored first on *a 42 yard field goal by Jorge Cimadevilla, then the Attack* would score the next 13 points. First on a one-yard run by WR/DB Darrell Philon, but the point after failed. Then, subbing quarterback Chris Parker threw a 46-yard touchdown pass to wr/db Alvin Williams. Orlando would score the next two touchdowns as an old friend returned to haunt Sacramento once again. This old friend was quarterback Ben Bennett, who was back after being released by the Surge just 14 months earlier. Bennett went right to work throwing two of his six touchdowns both to wr/db Barry Wagner. The first was a 25-yard strike followed by a seven-yard toss, giving Orlando a 17-13 lead.

The lead would change throughout the quarter, with Orlando scoring 17 points with Bennett throwing two more touchdowns. The first is mentioned above, the seven-yard pass to Wagner; the other was a 11 yard pass to rb/lb Jerry Odom. The Attack would score 13 points as well with the first coming off a 34 yard kick return by wr/db Niu Sale. Their second coming as qb Chris Parker tossed a three yarder to wr/db Darrel Philion for the final touchdown of the quarter. Orlando ended the scoring with a 34 yard field goal by Jorge Cimadevillia, giving the Predators a one-point lead 27-26 heading into the half.

As the third quarter began, so did Bennett as he led Orlando to 14 more points, widening the Predators lead by 15 points 41-26.

Bennett's first was a 36 yard pass to offense specialist Herkie Walls. The next touchdown was a five yard pass to Wagner (his third touchdown of the game). Sacramento's Chris Parker threw a 38 yard to Wayne Coffey closing the gap to 41-32 as the final quarter started.

After Cimadevillia kicked his third field goal from 21 yards out, Sacramento then got their offense moving for two more scores. Quarterback Parker connected with Coffey on both a 42 yard strike and a 10 yard toss, plus Parker threw a successful two point try as he connected with ol/dl Rich Ane. The Attack now held a slim three point lead 47-44. Bennett again connected with Wagner again. This one was from 11 yards out, giving Orlando a 51-47 lead. On the ensuing kick, The Attack miss handled the ball, and Wagner recovered it, running 11 yards for the final score of the game as the Predators won 58-47.

Wagner had five touchdowns, and Bennett threw for 237 yards and six touchdowns, while Sacramento's Chris Parker threw for 294 yards with five touchdowns as 6,061 fans were in attendance.

Game Three (at Arizona)

In their week three game in Arizona, the Attack would be playing another expansion team, the Rattlers. This game was played in the newly opened America West Arena, with 15,505 fans in attendance. The Rattlers scored first when Kicker Luis Zendejas kicked a 26 yard field goal. (Luis is from the famous football family).

After the field goal, Sacramento would score the next 22 points, starting with a 12 yard pass from Mike Hold to rb/lb Bart Schuchts, but the extra point was blocked. The Attack would score a safety on a blocked field goal as OL/DL Alo Sila got the credit for the block, making the score 9-3 in favor of Sacramento. The Attack would score again as WR/DB Darrell Philion returned a kickoff 57 yards, putting the Attack ahead 16-3. Then RB/LB Marshal Foreman (nephew to heavyweight champ George Foreman) scored on a two-yard run, giving the Attack a 22-3 lead.

The Rattlers would get back on the board as WR/DB Mike Richmond caught a 10 yard pass from Gene Johnson. Sacramento countered with a 2 yard run by WR/DB Richard Rodgers, giving the Attack a 29-10 lead late in the half. Arizona then began their comeback as QB Johnson scored on a 2 yard run and Zendejas booted a 40 yard field goal to end the half with Sacramento leading 29-17.

After the break, Arizona dominated the half, scoring the next 31 points starting with a one yard run by FB/LB David ELdrigde and Zendejas kicked a 43 yarder making the score 30-29 as the Rattlers defense held the Attack scoreless in the third quarter.

Arizona would score another three touchdowns in the final quarter the first was a 2 yard run by FB/LB Andy Coviella then a 8 yard pass from Johnson to WR/DB Ricki Lopez followed by a 40 yard run by FB/LB Art Greathouse, giving the Rattlers a 51-29 lead. The Attack would finally score on a 22 yard pass from Parker to RB/LB Bart Schuchts, making the final score 51-36 in favor of the Rattlers.

Game Four (at San Antonio)

So after three straight losses, the Attack got their first win, a 38-15 victory over division rival San Antonio with 11,688 fans in attendance inside HemisFair Arena in San Antonio. For the second week in a row, the Attack played another expansion team named the Force, who were one game ahead of Sacramento in the standings. Mike Hold got the Attack started when he threw a 27 yard pass to Wayne Coffey for the early 7-0 lead.

Then the Force would score the next 12 points, first on a 5 yard pass from qb Ken Lutz to wr James Harvey, then a 1 yard run by Lutz, but both extra point kicks failed, making the score 12-7 after one quarter.

The Attack regained the lead as Hold threw a 44 yard strike to wr/db Wayne Adkins, giving the Attack a 14 -12 lead. The Force would add a 46 yard field goal by Frantz, giving the Force their final lead 15-14, then Hold threw his third touchdown of the game to Coffey (his second) from 45 yards away as the Attack took control of the game scoring the next 17 points while their defense held San Antonio scoreless for the remainder of the game.

Sacramento's Hold threw his fourth touchdown to Coffey for his third score which came from 11 yards out, kicker Kevin Greene added a 25 yard kick in the fourth quarter before Hold threw his fifth touchdown to Bart Schuchts from 38 yards away to close out the scoring, giving the Attack a 38-15 win and a 1-3-0 record.

Game Five (Arizona)

The Attack returned home to face the Rattlers in their second meeting of the season with 6,215 fans on hand. These fans saw a very ugly game as it was marred by dropped passes, fumbles, and penalties, as both teams combined for only 98 total first-half yards.

The perfect example was the game's first score, which came as the Rattlers attempted a field goal that fell short and was returned by Sacramento's Wayne Adkins 55 yards for a touchdown. Arizona countered as FB/LB Andy Coviello scored on a 1 yard run, tying the game.

Moments later, the Attack took the lead for good as FB/LB Steve Jones scored from a yard away, giving the Attack a 14-7 halftime lead.

As the second half got started, so did Quarterback Hold, who found Adkins one more time with a 39-yard pass on their next series. Hold threw his second touchdown as he hit RB/LB Bart Schuchts from seven yards away. The score gave the Attack a 27-7 lead.

Arizona countered with a 43 yard touchdown pass from quarterback Gene Johnson to wr/db Cedric Tillman, cutting the Attack's lead to 13 points 27-14. The Rattlers would add a safety, making the score 27-16 yet this would be as close as Arizona would get as Sacramento scored on a 1 yard run by Hold, and with a successful 2 point pass (Hold to Adkins) the Attack had a 35–16 victory.

Mike Hold went 10 of 26 for 126 yards and two touchdowns, while Arizona's Gene Johnson went 13 of 32 for 163 yards and one touchdown. Sacramento was now 2-3-0 and in a tight three-way battle for first place.

Game Six (San Antonio)

To start the second half of the season, the Attack were hosting divisional rival San Antonio with 7,493 on hand and riding a two-game win streak. The visitors scored first with a 21-yard run by RB/LB James Greene, which turned out to be the only score of the quarter.

What happened next was nothing short of historic, as the Attack would score seven of the next eight touchdowns, with five of them coming before the Force could score their second. It all started as Hold threw the first of his five touchdowns when he found WR/DB Wayne Coffey from six yards away. (Coffey would catch two more scores, a 45 yard pass and a 28 yarder). Mike Hold would leave the game in the third quarter, not because of injury but only to rest after going 11 of 25 with 171 yards and five touchdowns.

Besides the three scores to Coffey, he threw a score to WR/DB Darrell Philon for 17 yards and another for 19 yards to WR/DB Wayne Adkins. The Attack also added a safety in the third, giving them a 44-14 lead heading into the final quarter.

With his team trailing by 30 points, Force quarterback Ken Lutz didn't give up as he led his team to three scores with two of them going to WR/DB Alvin Horn. The first was a 9 yarder, then a 45 yarder late in the quarter. Lutz also made a 7 yard toss to WR/QB James Harvey. Sacramento would add two more scores as well with backup quarter-back Chris Parker, who would throw a 8 yard score to Bart Schuchts and a 1 yard toss to OL/DL Joe March who was one of the carryover players from Denver. (March would beg coach Kapp for this play).

When the game was over, the Attack had a 65-35 victory, with the 65 points being the most Sacramento would score all season. The two teams combined for an even 100 points, and San Antonio's coach Dick Nolan refused to shake coach Kapp's hand after the game stating his team ran up the score, yet Kapp stated that his team might need the points for tiebreaker reasons for the playoffs.

Game Seven (at Charlotte)

Heading into their week seven game against the Rage inside the Charlotte Coliseum, the Attack were riding a three-game winning streak outsourcing their opponents 138–66 and very much in the playoff picture. This would be the first of a two-game East Coast trip for Sacramento (Detroit would be the other stop).

Pro football can be like a roller coaster, with ups and downs, and for the Attack, they had their ups, and now they were about to reach their lows. In this game, Charlotte would score first and often as they accounted for 51 of the 54 points that were scored. The Rage outplayed the Attack, who just couldn't execute, having three touchdowns nullified by either penalties or turnovers, as Sacramento had five turnovers, one fumble, and four interceptions.

Rage's quarterback Scooter Molander threw five touchdowns, four of which went to RB/LB Danny Smith, a seven-yard strike, then a 15 yarder, a 5 yard pass, and a 23 yard pass. The Rage would never lose the lead, scoring 31 straight points before the Attack would add their only points, a 57 yard field goal by Kevin Greene. Molander also threw a touchdown pass to WR/DB Ryan Bethea from 15 yards away. Charlotte also added a 45 yard field goal by Jim Power, a 2 yard run by RB/WR Les Barley, and then a fumble recovery in the end zone by WR/DB Eric Andrade to close out the scoring. The three points scored by Sacramento still rank second in the league's record books as the second-fewest points by one team. (San Antonio holds the record for being shutout in week six against Orlando 50-0).

The win snapped Charlotte's five-game losing streak and ended Sacramento's three game win streak as 11,598 fans watched.

Game Eight (at Detroit)

Following their disaster in Charlotte, the Attack was eager to get back on track in the Motor City. One strange note to this game was the fact that a printing error resulting in a few dozen tickets (at least) were issued to fans having Detroit hosting the L.A. Wings, and not the Attack. (some of these tickets can still be found on ebay). This game was played at the Joe Louis Arena with 14,710 fans in attendance.

Detroit scored first as quarterback Gilbert Renfroe ran in from one yard out. The Attack answered with a 33 yard field goal by Kevin Greene. The Drive would score again as Renfroe found WR/DB Gary Mullin with a 6 yard pass, ending the half with Detroit leading 14–3.

To begin the second half, the Drive scored as Renfroe found FB/LB Broderick Sargent with a 14 yard pass. The Attack finally found the end zone once again as Hold flipped a 1 yard pass to Wayne Coffey. This would be as close as the Attack would get as both their quarterbacks went down due to injuries. Sacramento would finish the game with a make-shift backfield of WR/DB Coffey, DB/WR Niu Sale, and kicker Kevin Greene.

Detroit would add 10 more points as Renfroe threw his third touchdown and second to Mullin from 40 yards away, then kicker John Langeloh added a 18 yard field goal. The lone bright spot from this game was that the Attack defense held the league's best offense to their lowest total all season allowing only 31 points in this game, yet the Attack still lost 31-10 as their offense continued to struggle.

Game Nine (Dallas)

The Attack returned home for a divisional game against the Texans, with both teams hoping to keep their playoff hopes alive.

This game was played at the Arco Arena with 8,226 fans in attendance. The game began with both teams kicking field goals as Sacramento scored on a 50 yarder,with the Texans trying the score with a 36 yarder. Sacramento scored the game's first touchdown on a 1 yard run by FB/LB Steve Jones just before the quarter ended.

Dallas added another 25 yard field goal to start the second quarter. Mike Hold scored on another 1 yard run, giving the Attack a 17–6 lead. The Texans finally found the end zone when QB Todd Hammel hit WR/DB Bobby Duncun with a 12 yard pass, but the two-point try failed. Dallas would record a safety when Hold was sacked in the end zone on third down following two incomplete passes, making the score 17-11 entering the half.

Sacramento opened the second half with a 18 yard touchdown pass from Hold to Wayne Coffey, giving the Attack a 24-11 edge. Dallas answered with two touchdowns; the first was a 41 yard bomb to WR/DB Gary Compton, then Hammel found WR/DB Tyrone Williams on a 19 yard strike. As the quarter ended, the Texans were now leading 28-24.

Sacramento failed on a fourth down play with the ball on the Dallas' 10 yard line. Then on the Texans first play Todd Hammel found an open man, but he was wearing an Attack jersey, as Zeph Lee returned his interception 21 yards for a touchdown, giving the Attack a 31-28 lead.

Todd Hammel then led his team down the field for the go-ahead score as FB/LB Dave Chapman would score from one yard out. Sacramento again took the lead as Hold connected with OL/DL Niu Sale on a 41 yard pass, giving the Attack a short-lived 38-34 lead. Dallas would score the game's final points as Hammel drove his team to the Attack 16 yard line before he threw his fourth touchdown pass to WR/DB Gary Compton (his second), giving Dallas a 41–38 win and putting Sacramento's playoff hopes in danger.

Game Ten (Cincinnati)

Coming into the final game of the season, Sacramento was hosting Cincinnati inside the Arco Arena with 9,021 fans on hand. The Attack needed to win this game and hope that at least two of these three teams would lose; Arizona, Cleveland, or Charlotte, so they would qualify. This game would be a wild roller coaster of a game.

Sacramento would open the scoring as Hold found Coffey with a 20 yard pass. The Rockers counted with a 7 yard score as QB Art Schlichter found RB/LB Tony Collins for the touchdown. Then, the Attack regained the lead with a 40 yard field goal by Greene. Schlichter put the Rockers ahead with a 33 yard pass to WR/DB Ira Hillary, making it 14-10 after one quarter.

Sacramento would turn up the heat in the second quarter as they outscored the visitors 28-6, starting with FB/LB Marshal Foreman's 3 yard run. Then on two separate touchdown passes from Hold to WR/DB Darrell Philon, the first was a 7 yarder followed by a 4 yard score. Schlichter then led his own scoring drive ending with a 3 yard pass to Hillary (his second).

The Attack then scored on a missed field goal try by the Rockers as DL/OL Jon Norris returned the loose ball two yards, ending the half with the home team leading 36–22.

Cincinnati would begin their comeback starting with a 26 yard pass from Schlichter to Collins (his second). The Rockers would score again as RB/LB Dan Sellers ran from two yards out, and with the successful two-point try, the game was knotted at 36. Sacramento would score just before the quarter's end as Mike Hold found Wayne Adkins on a 24 yard pass, but the kick failed. This would be a problem all game as both kickers missed seven extra points, four by the Attack and three by the Rockers, also Rockers kicker David Browndyke missed a field goal as well.

To start the final quarter, the Rockers scored on a 29 yard pass from Schlichter to WR/DB Todd Smith. The Attack countered with a 5 yard run on a lateral pass from Hold to Foreman; yet again, the two point try failed.

Cincinnati would tie the game once again as Schlichter threw a 14 yard pass to OL/DL Jackie Walker as the kick failed again leaving the game at 38, heading to overtime.

Sacramento won the coin toss and went right down scoring on their third play of the drive as Hold found Coffey once more with a 23 yard pass, and Greene made the kick. The Rockers got their chance to score, but the Attack's defense forced a four and out, giving Sacramento a 55–48 win and helping them to make the playoffs as Arizona lost to Dallas 33–20 and Charlotte lost 39–32 to Tampa Bay.

Both Cincinnati and Sacramento combined for 103 points, with 556 passing yards, as Mike Hold had 225 yards with five touchdowns, while Art Schlichter threw for 331 yards with seven touchdowns. The Attack would finish in second place at 4-6-0 and would face the Drive in Detroit in the first round of the playoffs.

Playoff Game (at Detroit)

In the first round of the playoffs Sacramento would be the seventh-seeded team facing the second-seeded Drive in Detroit. This game was played at the Joe Louis Arena, with 13,128 fans attending.

The Attack would take an early 10-0 lead as RB/LB Marshal Foreman (nephew of boxer George Foreman) would score on a 1 yard run, while Kevin Greene added a 40 field goal. Detroit answered with a 7 yard run by FB/LB Broderick Sargent, ending the first quarter.

Sacramento added a 32 yard field goal to begin the quarter. Drive qb Gil Renfroe found WR/DB Gary Mullen for a 17 yard touchdown, giving Detroit the lead for good as the Drive would score 13 more points before the half. First on a 30 yard field goal by John Langeloh followed by WR/DB George LaFrance's 4 yard catch from Renfroe.

Both teams traded field goals, with Kevin Greene kicking a 30 yarder for Sacramento and Detroit's John Langelgh adding a 25 yard kick, ending the first half with Detroit leading 26-16.

Detroit would control the half and the game as league MVP George LaFrance raced 57 yards with the opening kickoff for a touchdown. The Attack struck back as Hold found Wayne Coffey for a 35 yard touchdown, making the score 32–23 in favor of Detroit. The Drive would keep Sacramento scoreless for the remainder of the game while scoring another 16 points.

The first was a one yard run by B. Sargent followed by kicker Langeloh's third field goal from 20 yards. The game's final score came on a pass from Renfroe to Sargent (his third) from 10 yards away. Detroit won the game 48–23 to end the Attack's Cinderella season. After the season, the Kings ownership and Arco Arena chose not to purchase the Attack, leaving the league to find another buyer.

The team moved to Florida for the 1993 season, being called the Miami Hooters from 1993-1995 (named in part from an agreement with the restaurant chain). Then, following the '95 season the franchise moved to West Palm Beach and was renamed the Florida Bobcats from 1996–2001. Then, the team folded.

Remember, there is no chance any of this would have happened if the Wings cycling team had not filed their lawsuit.

The ATTACK...FINAL NOTES

- The Attack was the only team ran by the league until 2015 (New Orleans VooDoo and Las Vegas Outlaws)
- OL/DL player Alo Sila was named first team All-Arena

- OL/DL Joe March is the "ONLY" Attack player in the Arena League HOF (class of 2000) (former Surge and Arena QB Ben Bennett is in the hall class of 2000 as well)
- Head Coach Joe Kapp led the Minnesota Vikings to the last "official " NFL title in 1969 before losing to the K.C. Chiefs in Super Bowl IV. The NFL/AFL merger took place in 1970 with the former NFL becoming the NFC.

RECORDS (based on the 2013 record manual)

- Fewest yards in a game by one team: 42 yards 2nd all-time May 29,1992 @ Dallas (49--27 lost) page 192
- Most combined sacks one game: 11 total Sacramento– seven….San Antonio– four 1st all-time June 20,1992 @ San Antonio (38–15 win) page 194
- Fewest points by one team/game: 3 points 2nd all-time July 10,1992 @ Charlotte
- 2nd all-time fewest points by a road team (51–3 lost) page 191
- Fewest combined points game: 41 points 12th all-time July 17,1992 @ Detroit

Detroit 31 Sacramento 10 (lost) 10th all-time fewest points by road team (10) page seven 2019 postseason manual Online at Arenafan.com

POST SEASON RECORDS

- The game would be the last playoff game for the City of Sacramento, with the Attack losing 48–23.
- This game was played on August 8,1992 in Detroit
- Passing:
  1) Fewest pass completions one team: Sacramento (9)

2) Tied ; 2nd all-time page 206
3) Fewest pass completions combined: (24)
4) Detroit (15) Sacramento (9)
5) Tied; 1st all-time page 204
6) Fewest combined passing yards one game: (300 yards)
7) Detroit (194) Sacramento (106)
8) 3rd all-time page 206
9) Most sacks one game: (3.0)
10) Danny Lockett (Det.)
11) Tied 1st all-time page 204

- Field Goals: (3 Point Tries)
- All these records came from the game in Detroit on August 7,1992.
- Most attempts by one team/ game: (7)
- Tied; 2nd all-time Kevin Greene… Sacramento also listed in individual records pages 205 & 202.
- Most field goal attempts both teams (12) page 205
- 2nd all-time Sacramento (7) Detroit (5)
- Most field goals made both teams (6) page 205
- Tied; 3rd all-time Both teams had (3) each
- Most missed Field goal return yards combined (94)
- 3rd all-time Detroit 60 Sacramento 34 page 206

CFL '92 /'93

In February of 1992, pro football was in full bloom, playing year-round. The NFL had just finished their 72nd season with 28 teams; remember that Carolina, Jacksonville, the Ravens, and Texans were not in the league yet. The league was playing 16 games with three rounds of the playoffs, finishing with the Super Bowl. The NFL season starts in August and ends in February.

Next, there was the Professional Spring Football League or PSFL for short. This league was about to start its first season with 10 teams playing 10 games with the playoffs before ending with the "Red, White and Blue game." Their season was to run from February to June, but this league folded two weeks before their season started. Here is a list of the teams:

Arkansas Miners ,Carolina Cougars

Nevada Aces ,Miami Tribe

New Mexico Rattlesnakes, New England Blitz

Oregon Lightning Bolts ,Tampa Bay Outlaws

Utah Pioneers, Washington Marauders.

Next, there was the Arena Football League, which had just expanded to 12 teams, with three divisions tripling their original size. This league runs from May to August, playing 10 games and two rounds of playoff games ending with the Arena Bowl.

Finally, there was the World League of American Football or WLAF for short. This league was the brainchild and the spring league of the NFL with ten teams, playing ten games with one round of playoff games, ending with the World Bowl. The WLAF was just entering its second season, which runs from March to June, with teams in the States, Europe, and one in Canada making this league a true world league.

YES. American football was in full bloom, but up north Canadian football was struggling, with many teams facing major financial problems as the recession in Canada was starting to affect the teams, especially the eastern markets.

The Ottawa club was about to face competition from the Ottawa Senators, the NHL's newest team beginning play in the fall of 1992. To make matters worse, both Toronto and Hamilton started to worry about attendance due to the success of the NFL Buffalo Bills, who were in the midst of six straight playoff seasons, which included four straight Super Bowl appearances.

The CFL season starts in June and ends in November with eight teams playing 18 games, with two playoff games ending with the Grey Cup Championship. The cup is named after Canada's Governor General Earl Grey, who donated the trophy in 1909, hoping the trophy would be similar to the Stanley Cup.

Before the CFL, Canadian football had three rugby leagues. In the west, there was the "Western Interprovincial Football Union" or WIFU, which later became the Western Football Conference. The five teams were the Winnipeg Blue Bombers, the Calgary Stampeders, the Edmonton Eskimos, the Saskatchewan Roughriders, and the British Columbia Lions. In the east, there was the "Interprovincial Rugby Football Union" or simply the IRFU, which was also called the "Big Four." The four teams were the Hamilton Tiger-cats, the Montreal Alouettes, the Ottawa Rough Riders, and the Toronto Argonauts. (Montreal would fold in 1987 just before the start of the season as their financial problems were too much to continue. This would force Winnipeg to switch from the west to the east in order to balance the divisions.)

Finally, there was the "Ontario Rugby Football Union" or ORFU, which challenged for the Grey Cup until 1954 when the Union dropped out of the Grey Cup tournament to regroup, never to make it back.

Note: the ORFU had the "FIRST" American team to play Canadian-style football in 1956 when the Rochester Rockets joined the Union, playing five games before folding.

The Canadian Football League, or CFL, was formed on January 17, 1958, at the Royal Alexandra Hotel in Winnipeg as the two unions joined to form the CFL. While the CFL was formed in 1958, the last expansion came in 1954 when the British Columbia Lions joined the Western Interprovincial Football Union.

In the league's 34-year history (58–92), there were never more than nine teams, with just eight since Montreal folded in 1987. Yet in 1971, a group of investors from New York City, headed by Robert Schmentz, inquired about adding a new franchise in the city. Schmentz was a real estate developer and part owner of the NBA Portland Trail Blazers and Boston Celtics, and he later owned the WFL's New York Stars. His was one of two groups seeking a franchise for the city; the other was led by singer Paul Anka, who was born in Ottawa and as stated he was still a Canadian.

Both groups looked into whether Yankee Stadium could be converted to suit a CFL franchise because the NFL Giants were supposed to move into Giants Stadium in 1972, leaving Yankee Stadium without a football tenant. The move would not happen until 1976. The CFL received his letter on November 26, 1971; along with his letter, league comissioner, Jake Gaudaur, received other letters inquiring about possible franchises in Chicago, Indianapolis, Georgia, and Mexico City. One other group that was also very interested was the group from Detroit, for the same reason as the two N.Y. groups, as the NFL Lions did not want to move to Downtown, rather they chose to move into the Pontiac Silverdome. (Again, no names or groups were ever mentioned.)

Seven months later, in May of 1972, a general meeting was held for the league at which time the chairman noted that several press reports indicated considerable criticism for the fact that the league erred in failing to expand into the states. (Again, no names or places were mentioned concerning this meeting.)

In 1983, the city of Halifax, Nova Scotia, was granted a "Conditional" expansion team making them the 10th team in the league. Halifax was to begin play in 1984 and would be called the Atlantic Schooners. So what was the condition? The team had to build a suitable stadium and have secure ownership in place by early 1984. None of this happened, and the application was withdrawn. The city would be granted another franchise to begin play in 2020, but Covid-19 put their plans on hold. This new team chose the same name as the first club.

Next up was a rumor story printed in the Orlando Sentinel paper on January 24, 1987, reporting that a possible merger between the CFL and dominant USFL was in the works. According to the brief story, Arizona Outlaws Coach Frank Kush approached CFL Comissioner Doug Mitchell about a merger of the two leagues. Kush stated that he discussed the idea with several CFL officials at the 1987 Senior Bowl. Former USFL Comissioner Harry Usher knew nothing about this rumor but was open to a meeting, and Mitchell was leery but open as well. Below is an idea of what the league could have looked like had the merger happened:

CFL Conference	USFL Conference
East Division	Independence Division
Toronto Argonauts	Arizona Outlaws
Hamilton Tiger-cats	Jacksonville Bulls
Ottawa Rough Riders	Orlando Renegades
Montreal Alouettes	Tampa Bay Bandits
West Division	Liberty Division
British Columbia Lions	Baltimore Stars
Calgary Stampeders	Birmingham Stallions

Edmonton Eskimos   Memphis Showboats

Saskatchewan Roughriders   New Jersey Generals

Winnipeg Blue Bombers

Then, most recently, in March of 2021, after Dwayne "The Rock" Johnson purchased the second XFL, he met with CFL officials to discuss a possible merger after Covid-19 ended both of their seasons, which caused the XFL to fold. After one month of meetings with little results, both sides agreed to end the talks.

So why did the CFL not expand into the states sooner? Was it because the league played a different style of football which included 12 men per side, three downs instead of four or because their field is wider and longer? (see the chart) Whatever the reason, the league just never seemed to welcome the idea of moving into the States until 1992. But it now seemed to be the right time if there was the right man to oversee this move. Was Larry Smith that man?

On February 27, 1992, Larry Smith became the ninth comissioner of the CFL at the age of 41. Although he was appointed as the comissioner on this date, it was not until April 1, 1992, that he officially took office. His first order of business was to stop the ship from sinking. As stated previously, the league was in serious trouble with some teams facing shut down.

Smith was used to getting results and was no stranger to the league. Born in 1951, a native of Hudson, Quebec, Smith graduated with a degree in economics from Bishops University. He then went on to play for Montreal in 1972, being the team's number-one pick that year. He went on to play nine seasons for the Alouettes from 1972 to 1980 as a halfback/slotback. During his career Smith played in 122 consecutive regular season games, 13 straight playoff games, and five Grey Cups, 140 consecutive in all. During his career, Montreal made the playoffs nine straight seasons, going to five Grey Cup games, winning two of them in 1974 and 1977. The Alouettes also played in three straight Cup games from 1977-79, winning in '77.

With Smith, the Alouettes' record was 85-67-6, with three division titles. So in summing all this up, Smith knew how to get results. After his playing days, Smith began his business career with positions in sales, marketing, and human resources. In 1983, he joined Industrial Life Technical Services as general manager of the Montreal branch. The following year, he assumed responsibility for the multi-products division. In 1985, Smith became the senior vice president of the central region. Between 1985 and 1991, Smith held several positions with various divisions of John Labatt LTD. Most recently was president of the frozen bakery division of Ogilvie Mills LTD.

Mr Smith was well-suited to be league comissioner, for he had a vision for the league, which was to have 20 teams, with 10 teams in Canada and 10 teams in the States.

On June 25, 1992, Smith took the first step towards his vision when he scheduled a preseason game to be played in Portland, Oregon. This would be the first CFL game in the States since July 9, 1967, when the B.C. Lions defeated the Edmonton Eskimos 7–2 in Everett, Wash, with 6,248 fans in Everett Memorial Stadium.

For the 1992 game, two old-time rivals were chosen to take part in this event as the Toronto Argonauts and the Calgary Stampeders faced off inside Portland Civic Stadium with 15,362 fans on hand. Calgary defeated Toronto 20–1, as the Argonauts' only points came on the rogue.

Since his arrival in February, Smith had already laid the foundation for his vision. With the test game over, he could now go onto the next step…expansion, but first, he had to fix the current money problems.

With two parts of the triathlon now complete, we need to set the stage for the final part. During the '92 Arena League season, the owners of the WLAF clubs had to wait three months for the

September NFL owners meeting to see if there would be a 1993 season, just like they had to wait and see about the 1992 season. Then, on September 18, 1992, the NFL owners voted to table the WLAF and bring it back as an all-European league in 1995. This left the owners of the seven North American teams wondering what to do next. Three of the owners decided to sue the NFL for breach of contract because when they first joined the spring league in 1991, they were guaranteed a three-year deal to join, yet after two seasons, the NFL owners tabled the league. These three owners were Fred Anderson of Sacramento, Larry Benson of San Antonio, and Roger Dore` of Montreal. This lawsuit would take almost three months to settle.

During the wait, these three owners decided to talk to Larry Smith about joining the CFL. Now, the CFL was in the middle of its 1992 season when the announcement came that the NFL had suspended the World League of American Football. This news gave Smith hope and an open door to expand into the states with three willing owners. Only one question remains: did the NFL leave the door open for Smith and the CFL to expand into the states? I believe the answer is YES! By suspending the WLAF, the NFL left these owners still wanting more football.

Roughly after two-plus months in court, the NFL owners and the owners of the North American teams from the WLAF settled the lawsuit for an undisclosed amount, which Surge owner Fred Anderson stated was below the three million he was seeking. Anderson was hoping to use the NFL money to pay the expansion fee to join the CFL, but he would need some help in order to field his team in 1993. Speaking about expansion teams, the CFL had narrowed the field to four cities which were Sacramento, San Antonio, Montreal, and Portland. The first three were former WLAF cities and their owners. The Portland bid was placed by Paul Allen, who was co-founder of Microsoft Corporation. Yet Montreal's

Roger Dore` would be the first to fold in November as he could not find any partners. This answers the question of why Montreal never joined the CFL after playing in the WLAF.

On January 12, 1993, Larry Smith and the CFL made their historic announcement that Sacramento and San Antonio were granted franchises for the 1993 season. It would be on January 19 that Paul Allen withdrew his bid for a team in Portland; only four years later, he would own the NFL Seattle Seahawks.

With the addition of San Antonio and Sacramento, the CFL now had 10 teams for the FIRST time in league history. Yet these 10 teams lasted about two weeks, for on January 28, 1993, San Antonio owner Larry Benson announced that he was withdrawing from the league, stating financial reasons as the cause. Benson hoped to field a team in 1994, yet this never happened.

Smith was now down to just nine teams, with only one in the states. Anderson was able to keep the colors from the Surge, yet the nickname was the property of the NFL. Anderson decided to call his team the Gold Miners, which was fitting as the CFL was hoping to find gold in California with Sacramento. Anderson could have called his team the Scouts, Pioneers, or even Explorers as they were an experimental team bringing a new brand of football into the states, yet not just any state but California, a state with four NFL teams at that time.

Anderson was happy to have a team in a league with some history and finally have all the problems of the last couple of months behind him. His team and he were ready to get back to the business of football.

KEY NOTES:

- Sacramento became the first expansion team in the history of the league (1958-1992).
- Larry Smith had a vision for a 20-team league with 10 teams in Canada and 10 in the States.

- Fred Anderson refused to give up on his dream of owning a pro football team.
- There was interest in 1971 from a group in New York City to join the CFL.
- A rumor in 1987 that the USFL wanted to merge with the CFL but it fell through.
- Microsoft co-founder Paul Allen almost joined the CFL.
- The Montreal Alouettes first folded in 1982, just before the start of the season, but a new owner was found. This owner changed the name to Concordes in honor of the giant aircraft. After four seasons, he changed the name back to the Alouettes, hoping to increase fan support, which failed, and the team folded for good in 1987.

SAN ANTONIO (91–92)

Let us step away from Sacramento for a moment to pay tribute to the triathlon runner-up. The city of San Antonio also had a team in the WLAF called the Riders, owned by Larry Benson, brother of Tom Benson, the New Orleans Saints owner. The team was coached by Mike Riley, who went on to coach the then San Diego Chargers from 1999-2001. The Riders also had a Hall of Fame coach as their general manager, Tom Landry and his son Tom Jr.

In 1991, Riley coached the Riders to a second-place finish in the West division with a 4-6-0 record. Then, in '92, he coached them to a 7-3-0 Record, yet they finished in third (last) place in their division, missing the playoffs both seasons. Their home field was Alamo Stadium in '91 and Bobcat Stadium in '92, which was 45 miles outside of San Antonio.

San Antonio had an 11-9-0 overall record for both seasons and oddly went 5-5-0 on the road. The team also had some highly noted names on their squad, like quarterback Jason Garrett, who not only played for the Cowboys but went on to be their head coach from 2011-2019. Then there was John Layfield Bradshaw, who played right tackle for the Riders in 1991 before going on to make a career in the WWE as "JBL."

Just like Sacramento, San Antonio would have an Arena team in 1992 as well called the Force. While Sacramento's Arena team made the playoffs, the Force finished last in their division and second last overall with a 2-8-0 record. The Force played their home games at the HemisFair Arena in San Antonio and has the honor of being the ONLY team to be shutout in an Arena League game, losing 50–0 to the Orlando Predators on June 13, 1992. This loss was the start of a five game losing streak that saw the Force being outscored 240–92, with the first three games totaling only 22 points.

Benson also sued the NFL over the WLAF folding and decided to join the CFL. Benson's team was to be called the San Antonio Texans, yet just two weeks after joining the CFL, Benson told the league he could not field his team in 1993. He hoped to have his team ready for the '94 season; this, of course, never happened.

So on January 29, 1993, when Benson announced that his club was suspending operations, not only did he kill his dreams and those of the city of San Antonio, but he also caused the city to drop out of the Pro Football Triathlon after finishing two-thirds of it. San Antonio would get their CFL team two years later when the Gold Miners would move to the city after stadium problems in Sacramento, taking the name Texans in 1995. More on this team later.

KEY NOTES:

- Only team to be shutout, losing 50–0 to Orlando on June 13, 1992 (a record for fewest points by one team).
- Most sacks in an Arena game, both teams with 11 Sacramento (7) and San Antonio (4) on June 20, 1992.
- The Force had three kickers in their brief season which combined to make only four field goals of the 34 attempts on the season.
- Played in the only tie game in WLAF history, a 17-17 at London on Saturday, April 11, 1992.
- The Texans, for a team that lasted only two weeks, had two different helmets and logos. The first was a silver helmet with a banner type flag with a star and a design of the Alamo at the bottom. The other was the more visual white helmet with the Texas flag. Both designs are pictured.

JL0717 GA   GEN ADM C   8.00
EVENT CODE   SECTION   ROW   SEAT   INCL. CITY SERV. FEE
$ 8.00   GEN. ADMISSION $
INCL. CITY SERV. FEE
GA   **
SECT   DETROIT DRIVE
GA 155X   VS
                 LOS ANGELES WINGS
GEN ADM   JOE LOUIS ARENA
ROW   SEAT   FRI JULY 17, 1992 8:00PM

SAN ANTONIO
TEXANS

NFL // CFL field measurements

The NFL field is 100 yards long by 53 ⅓ wide, with the midfield at the 50 yard line. The end zones are 10 yards deep, making the total length at 120 yards in all.

The CFL field is 110 yards long by 65 yards, with the midfield at the 55 yard line. The CFL end zones are 20 yards deep, making the total length at 150 yards in all.

Just like how different the fields are in each league, so too are the placement of the goal posts…while the NFL places the posts at the back of the end zone the CFL places them in the front of the end zone. The CFL states that this allows for the kickers to have the same distance as NFL kickers.

The goal posts for each of these two leagues are 18.5 feet wide with the cross bar at 10 feet in height.

Arena field measurements

The indoor football field is 85 feet wide with a padded surface and are 50 yards in length with 8 yard end zones at each end. Goal posts are 9 feet wide with a crossbar set at 15 feet in height.

The goalside rebound nets are 30 feet wide by 32 feet high. The bottom of the nets are 8 feet above the ground. The sideline barriers are 4 high and made of high density foam rubber.

The NFL third place game 1961–1970

1961; Detroit Lions- 17 Cleveland Browns- 16

1962; Det. Lions–38 Philadelphia Eagles-10

1963; Det. Lions– 17 Pittsburgh Steelers–10

1964; G.B. Packers-43 Cleveland Browns –20

1965; St. Louis Cards-24 G.B.Packers– 17

1966;Baltimore Colts-35 Dallas Cowboys–3

1967; Balt. Colts-20 Phila. Eagles –14

1968; L.A. Rams –30 Clev. Browns –6

1969; Da. Cowboys–17 Minnesota Vikings–13

1970; L.A. Rams –31 Dallas Cowboys –0

After the NFL/AFL merger this game was no longer played.

CFL '93 Part I

Game One (at Ottawa)

After five months of planning and lawsuits, it was now time to play football. Not just any football, but CFL football which was the final stage of the Pro Football Triathlon. On Wednesday, July 7, 1993, the Sacramento Gold Miners headed north to Ottawa, Canada's capital, to play the Rough Riders at Frank Clair Stadium with 23,916 fans on hand to witness this historic event. The Gold Miners had won both of their preseason games, first a 21-15 victory over Winnipeg, then a 32-20 win over the B.C. Lions.

Ottawa controlled the first quarter, jumping out to a 14-0 lead as Ottawa's quarterback Tom Burgess threw the first of his three scores, an 11-yard toss to wide receiver Stephen Jones. Then Jones would throw a touchdown pass of 46 yards to receiver Wayne Walker, and kicker Terry Baker added both converts, making the score 14-0 after the first quarter. Sacramento got on the board with 56 seconds left in the half when Dave Archer threw his first touchdown as he connected with running back Mike Oliphant on an eight yard pass. Ottawa answered 34 seconds later as Burgess threw his second touchdown of the game, a 61-yard bomb to receiver Jack Climie, ending the half with the home team leading 21-7.

The Gold Miners scored first in the second half as Oliphant jetted 45 yards to the end zone, narrowing the Rough Riders lead to seven points 21-14. Ottawa answered as Burgess threw his third touchdown, a 44-yard pass to Walker, his second of the game. The Gold Miners would close out the quarter, scoring eight points as Archer connected with receiver Willie Bouyer with an 18-yard toss. Then kicker Jim Crouch added the convert and a single when he missed a 43 field goal. The final quarter was all Ottawa as they outscored Sacramento 4-1, starting with Rough Riders kicker Baker booting a 37-yard field goal. The Gold Miners got a single when Ottawa's returner Anthony Drawhorn conceded on a 41-yard missed field goal try by Crouch. Then Baker missed a 34-yard try, giving the single to Ottawa to close out the scoring and giving Ottawa a 32-23 victory in this history-making game. Sacramento was now in the record books for being the first American team to play an official CFL game in Canada. Sacramento made the record books as the FIRST (and Only) Pro Football Triathlon City. Three different styles of football in three different leagues with three different rules. Ottawa made the record books for being the first city to host an official CFL game between two countries.

Game Two (at Hamilton)

For their second game of the season, the Gold Miners were in Hamilton to play the Tiger-cats in front of 20,307 spectators. This game was played at Ivor Wynne Stadium less than 72 hours after their inaugural CFL game in Ottawa. The Tiger-cats opened the scoring as quarterback Don McPherson found wide receiver Earl Winfield with a 25-yard touchdown pass and, with a successful convert, put Hamilton ahead 7-0 as the two teams headed into the second quarter. The Gold Miners would score a single as their kicker Jim Crouch missed a 45-yard field goal (Crouch missed three kicks in Ottawa), then roughly three minutes later, Crouch connected on a 35-yard kick. Next Tiger-cats kicker Paul (Ozzie) Osbaldiston booted the first of his three field goals from 11 yards away to end the half.

Sacramento opened the second half scoring with a 17-yard field goal by Crouch for his second of the game. Late in the quarter, the Miners were driving for their first touchdown when Hamilton's defensive back Gary Wilkerson stepped in front of Archer's pass and returned it 45 yards for the score, ending the Gold Miners threat and giving Hamilton a 17-7 lead. Heading into the final quarter, Archer again was moving the ball down field only to have Wilkerson step in front of his pass once more, ending the threat once again. Hamilton's McPherson took advantage of the turnover as he threw a 56-yard touchdown pass to receiver Scott Walker putting the game out of reach with the score 24-7. About six minutes later, Ti-cats Osbaldiston kicked his second field goal, a 27-yarder. Archer then led the Miners to their only touchdown of the game with just a little more than a minute left in the game as he found receiver Rod Harris with a five-yard pass. Crouch added the convert to make the score 27-14 in favor of Hamilton.

With 26 seconds left to play, Ozzie kicked his third of the game, a 44-yarder to end the scoring, giving Hamilton a 30-14 victory. Sacramento would have to wait at least one more game to become the first U.S. team to win an official CFL game, as they lost their first two games. Both teams combined for 618 yards of total offense, the lowest of the season. Archer was not having fun so far as he was sacked 12 times, throwing just three touchdowns with five interceptions and 559 passing yards in two games. Yet the good news was that the Miners were heading home.

Game Three (CALGARY)

Once again history was in attendance as the defending Grey Cup champions, Calgary Stampeders, visited Hornet Stadium to play the Gold Miners with 20,082 spectators in the stands. This was the first "OFFICIAL" CFL game played in the U.S. between an American and a Canadian team. This game was a shootout as the two teams combined for 74 points. The Miners opened the scoring as Crouch kicked an 11-yard field goal; less than three minutes later, the Stampeders tied the score when their kicker Mark McLoughlin kicked a 15-yarder. He would go on to score the next four points. First was a 27-yard field goal, then about three minutes later, he added a single when he missed a field goal try. Sacramento then started the game's longest drive of 11 plays covering 80 yards, ending with running back Robert Hardy's one-yard run followed by the successful convert. The

Miners now led 10-7. Crouch would add a single and a 22-yard field goal. Calgary's McLoughlin would add a 20-yard kick to finish the scoring in the first half, with Sacramento ahead 14-10.

The second half got started so did Calgary quarterback Doug Flutie, as he led the Stampeders to 21 straight points, all touchdown passes, with the first being a 37-yard pass to slotback Allen Pitts, next was a 14-yard toss to receiver Will Moore, then a five-yard pass to slotback David Sapunjis. The Gold Miners scored with just 39 seconds left in the quarter as Archer connected with receiver Rod Harris on a nine-yard pass. The Gold Miners went on to score two more touchdowns to take a 35-31 lead as running back Mike Oliphant scored from eight yards away. Then Archer found receiver Willie Bouyer with a 12-yard strike. Flutie then moved the Stampeders 78 yards in six plays, with the last play a three-yard run by Flutie giving Calgary a 38-35 lead.

Sacramento's Crouch scored a single as his 40-yard attempt went wide to end the scoring and the game, with Calgary clinging to a 38-36 victory. Both quarterbacks combined for 875 yards with five touchdowns as Flutie went 24 of 41 for 428 yards with three touchdowns, while Archer went 33 of 47 for 447 yards and two touchdowns with one interception and one sack.

Game Four (Saskatchewan)

This game turned out to be historic in many ways. First, the Gold Miners jumped out to a 24-0 lead in front of the 17,319 fans at Hornet Stadium. Archer opened the scoring as he found Mike Oliphant for a 33-yard touchdown, and then he connected with receiver Carl Parker on an eight-yard pass to end the quarter. Twenty-two seconds into the next quarter, Archer connected with receiver Titus Dixon for a franchise-record 90-yard touchdown pass. Kicker Crouch added a 37-yard field Goal, then Roughrider quarterback Kent Austin began the comeback as he threw a 36 yard pass to slotback Jeff Fairholm. Austin then ran the ball in from one yard out to cut the Miners' lead to ten points as both teams traded field goals to end the half, with Crouch kicking a 20-yarder and Ridgway kicking a 39-yarder for the Roughriders. With the score 27-17 Sacramento, the third quarter was all Saskatchewan as kicker Ridgway kicked three field goals. The first was a 24-yarder, then a 14-yarder, and a 32-yarder, giving Ridgway four field goals on the day, and Crouch added a 34-yard kick, putting the score at 30-26. Mike Pringle sealed the win for the Gold Miners with a 25-yard run, giving his team their first win in their inaugural CFL season, 37-26.

In this game, both quarterbacks attempted 90 passes with 779 yards, and for the first time all season, Archer did not have an interception, while Austin had three. Archer was sacked three times, bringing the season total to 15 in just four games. Also, this was the first game the Miners had the lead and never lost it and became the first American football team to win an official CFL game against a Canadian team.

Game Five (Edmonton)

This game was the third straight home game for the Miners, with 17,827 fans in attendance at Hornet Stadium. After earning their first win a week earlier, the Miners were hoping to extend the streak. The Eskimos scored first as kicker Sean Fleming booted a 34-yarder. Crouch then kicked his eighth of the season from 26 yards away. This would be as close as the Gold Miners would get to winning as Edmonton would score 23 points in the second quarter, starting with Fleming kicking two more field goals, a 19-yarder and a 45-yarder. Next, fullback Blake Marshall scored two straight touchdowns, first a five-yard dash, then he caught a six-yard pass from quarterback Glenn Harper. On the final play of the half, Fleming added his fourth field goal of the game, a 58-yard kick, giving the Eskimos a 26-3 lead.

Sacramento added a single when Crouch missed a 43-yard attempt to open the second half scoring. On the Miners' next series, Archer fumbled in the end zone, with Edmonton's linebacker Bernie

Goods recovering for the score. With the Eskimos ahead 33-4, Archer was replaced by Kerwin Bell, who led the Miners to their only touchdown, an eight-yard pass to receiver Rod Harris. This would be Sacramento's final score, as the Eskimos would score 10 more points. First was an 18-boot by Fleming followed by a 59-yard pass from Damon Allen to receiver Trent Brown, giving Edmonton a 43-11 victory. Both of the Miners' quarterbacks were sacked seven times, bringing the season total to 22 sacks in just five games, while Archer threw three interceptions giving him nine on the season with only seven touchdowns. This game was the team's worst defeat so far, as they lost by 32 points.

Game Six (at Toronto)

Coming into this game, Toronto still did not have a win, while the Gold Miners wanted to get back into the win column. This game was played at the Skydome in Toronto with 28,612 fans in attendance. Halfway through the first quarter, the Argos quarterback Mike Kerrigan threw a 32-yard pass to receiver Paul Masotti to open the scoring. Sacramento wasted little time scoring as running back Mike Oliphant raced 52 yards to tie the score. Just before the quarter's end, Argonauts kicker Lance Chomyc connected on a 24-yard field goal. Toronto would score two more times in the second quarter, both touchdown passes from Kerrigan. First was a seven-yard toss to slotback Kip Lewis, then a 15-yard pass to Masotti, his second of the game. As the half was winding down, Miners' Crouch attempted a 40 field goal but missed, giving the Miners a single, making the score 24-8 at the break in favor of Toronto.

The third quarter would be the quietest one of the game as Toronto padded their lead when running back Derrick McAdoo scored from one yard out. Sacramento countered with a 29-yard boot by Crouch, ending the quarter. As the fourth quarter got underway, the Argos added to their lead as Chomyc kicked his second field goal from 18 yards away. With the score 34-11, it appeared the game was out of reach; then Crouch kicked his second field goal from 37 yards away, while Sacramento scored two straight touchdowns, the first was a 59-yard punt return by slotback Freeman Baysinger for the score, next Oliphant rambled in from four yards out. Suddenly, this was a game once again as the Miners trailed by nine, 34-25. With less than a minute to play, Toronto added to their lead as Chomyc kicked his third of the day from 33 yards away. Once again, his kick seemed to seal the win for the Argos, but Archer had a final chance to steal the win as he led his team down the field in seven plays, ending with a two-yard pass from Archer to Harris, leaving only a second on the clock. The Gold Miners staged a great comeback, yet in the end, Toronto hung on to earn their first win of the season, 37-35.

The game was another quarterback duel as Toronto's Kerrigan threw for 467 yards, going 32 of 49 with three touchdowns and four interceptions. Archer went 29 of 47 for 345 and one touchdown with one interception while being sacked five times. Sacramento cornerback Kip Texada earned defensive player of the week for his one interception and several solo tackles.

Game Seven (Hamilton)

For the seventh game of the season, the Gold Miners returned home to Hornet Field with the smallest crowd of the season, 14,656 spectators on hand. The Miners played host to the Tiger-cats. In a solid all-around team performance, Sacramento scored 15 straight points as Archer threw two of his three touchdowns, the first to Baysinger from 31 yards out, capping a six-play 66-yard drive. Next, Archer connected with Parker on a 25-yard strike, ending a five-play, 55-yard drive. Sacramento's punter Paul McJulien got in on the action when he recorded a single on a 46-yard punt. Hamilton finally got on the board when kicker Paul Osbaldiston booted a 25-yard field goal, ending the quarter.

Miner's kicker Crouch added the first of his three field goals, a 25-yarder, then Miners' linebacker Paschall Davis stepped in front of

Tiger-cat's Don McPhenson's pass and returned it 39 yards for the score, making it 25-3 with just four minutes gone in the second quarter. Crouch then kicked his next two field goals of the game, with the first from 13 yards and his third from 31 yards as the half drew near, with Sacramento leading 31-3.

After the break, Sacramento continued to score as Crouch earned a single, missing a 46-yard field goal. Archer then threw his third and final touchdown of the day, a 30-yard pass to Baysinger. The Gold Miners running back Oliphant scored on a four-yard run that ended a nine-play drive that covered 92 yards. The Tiger-cats finally scored as receiver Earl Winfield caught a 15-yard pass from backup quarterback Eros Sanchez with no time left on the clock. The only bad part of this 46-10 win was that Archer was sacked five times, raising the season total to 32. Archer finished the game going 22 of 38 for 370 yards with three touchdowns and no interceptions. Both of Hamilton's quarterbacks combined for only 166 passing yards with one touchdown, three interceptions, and two sacks.

Game Eight (Winnipeg)

The Blue Bombers were coming into Sacramento after losing three days earlier to B.C. 48-28, while the Miners were coming off their best game so far after defeating Hamilton 46-10. Winnipeg opened the scoring as kicker Troy Westwood connected on three field goals, with two of them in the first quarter, a 12-yarder followed by one from 23 yards away. Westwood then kicked a 29-yarder to start the second quarter. The Bombers added to their lead when quarterback Matt Dunigan hit slotback Gerald Wilcox with a 13-yard pass to give Winnipeg a 17-0 lead.

Trailing by three scores, Archer began the comeback. First, Crouch gained a single when he missed a 49-yard attempt followed by a 12-yard field goal. About 60 seconds later, Archer connected with running back Oliphant on a 78-yard touchdown pass making the score 17-11. Winnipeg needed to regain control when Dunigan threw his second touchdown of the game, a 10 yard pass to wide receiver Dave Williams with five seconds left in the half.

After a scoreless third quarter, Dunigan threw his third touchdown of the game to Williams again from 34 yards out. Now trailing 30-11, Archer and Oliphant connected for their second score, which was a 69-yard bomb with under three minutes left to play. Sacramento's comeback fell short, leaving 15,509 spectators feeling let down. Archer threw a career-high 496 yards, going 26 of 42 with two touchdowns and three interceptions, along with two sacks. The season total was now at 37 in just eight games. Archer also threw to seven different receivers in this game. The Gold Miners' 536 total yards were their second-best output of the season.

Game Nine (at Saskatchewan)

The Gold Miners approached the midway point of the season with a 2-6-0 record and looking for their third win of the season. Sacramento traveled to Saskatchewan to play the Roughriders in front of the largest crowd in team history, as 33,032 fans filled Taylor Field. (Founded in 1910, Saskatchewan had to wait 83 years to play in front of their largest home crowd.)

After a scoreless first quarter, the Gold Miners would control most of the second as Archer connected with Rod Harris on a 14-yard pass. In less than three minutes, Archer found Oliphant with a 16-yard pass, then Crouch added two singles as he first missed a 67-yard try, and then he missed a 38-yard attempt. Trailing 16-0, the Roughriders needed to score before the half to stay in the game, which they did as kicker Dave Ridgway booted a 48-yarder with 46 seconds left in the half.

Saskatchewan opened the second half scoring just 43 seconds into the half as quarterback Kent Austin found slotback Ray Elgaard with a 27-yard pass for the score. Crouch added another single when he missed a 40-yard attempt. The Gold Miners got two more field goals from Crouch to end the Quarter, the first from 22 yards and the second from 21 yards away. Now leading 23-10, the Gold Miners' hopes of victory were looking good.

Shortly into the final quarter, the Roughriders began their comeback hopes as Austin found receiver Donald Narcisse with a 23-yard pass for the score. This would be the Riders' last touchdown. Trailing 23-17, Ridgway began to kick away at the Miners' lead, as he kicked three more field goals from 27, 46, and 30 yards away, with the last kick splitting the uprights as the gun sounded giving the Roughriders a 26-23 victory.

Archer finished the game completing 25 of 40 passes for 327 yards with two touchdowns and one interception. And for the first time all season Archer was not sacked. Heading into the second half of the season, the Gold Miners were at the bottom of their division with two wins and seven losses. Kicker Jim Crouch led the league in singles (rouges) with 12 and was fifth in scoring with 86 points. Running back Mike Oliphant was in tenth place in scoring with 10 touchdowns.

Here are some highlights from the first half of the season:

- The first U.S. team to play an "Official " CFL game in Canada, July 7, 1993 (32-23 lost to Ottawa in Ottawa).
- First U.S. team to host an "Official" CFL game in the U.S. between two different countries, July 17, 1993, 38-36 lost to Calgary in Sacramento, CA.
- First U.S. team to defeat a Canadian team in an "official" CFL game, July 21, 1993, 37-26 win over Saskatchewan in Sacramento, CA.
- Played in front of a record crowd of 33,032 fans in Saskatchewan. (Largest crowd in team history.)
- David Archer, in nine games, completed 232 of his 373 passes for 3,133 yards with 15 touchdowns and 14 interceptions and being sacked 37 times (this is NOT a record).

- Played in front of the smallest home crowd of the season on August 14, 1993, with 14,656 fans in attendance.

CFL '93 Part II

Game Ten (at Edmonton)

To open the second half of the season, the Gold Miners traveled to Edmonton to play the Eskimos at Commonwealth Stadium in front of the largest home crowd all season, as 37,042 fans packed in to see this game. The Eskimos opened the scoring as quarterback Damon Allen ran the ball in himself from two yards out. About nine minutes later, Edmonton kicker Sean Fleming booted a 14-yard field goal to make the score 10-0 after the first quarter.

The Gold Miners got on the board when punter Pete Gardere kicked a 63-yard punt for the single, and then Crouch added a 42-yard field goal to end the half with the Miners trailing 10-4. After playing through a scoreless third quarter, Fleming kicked a 37-yard field goal to increase Edmonton's lead to 13-4. Archer would throw his only touchdown of the game, a one-yard toss to Rod Harris with less than two minutes left in the game. On the ensuing kickoff, Crouch recorded a single when his kick traveled 85 yards into the end zone, making the final score 13-12 as the Eskimos ran out the clock.

This game saw the second-lowest combined offensive output all season, as both teams had just 627 yards of total offense combined. Allen went 15 of 28 for 196 yards, with no touchdowns and two interceptions while Archer went 20 of 38 for 236 yards, with one touchdown and two interceptions. Both quarterbacks were sacked three times apiece, and the Eskimos had almost 12 minutes more of possession, which hindered the Miners' offense.

One final note: Edmonton's Henry Gizmo Williams would break the all-time punt return yardage record as he returned seven punts for 113 yards, giving him 6,427 return yards. The previous record was 6,350 yards which was held by Paul Bennett while playing for

Toronto, Winnipeg, and Hamilton.

Game Eleven (Ottawa)

Sacramento played host to the Ottawa Rough Riders at Hornet Field with 16,510 fans in attendance. The Miners would score first as running back Mike Pringle ran the ball in from one yard out, then Ottawa answered as quarterback Tom Burgess connected with receiver Shawn Daniels from six yards away. This would be as close as the Riders would get to winning as Crouch kicked a 23-yard field goal just as the quarter ended.

Sacramento then added to their lead less than five minutes into the second quarter as Mike Oliphant raced 22 yards to make the score 17-7. Ottawa countered as Burgess scored from five yards away, and kicker Terry Baker added a single less than two minutes later. With less than 15 seconds left in the half, Archer added to the Miners lead as he threw a 49-yard bomb to receiver Joe Johnson to end the first half scoring, giving the Miners a 24-15 lead at the break.

The second half was all Sacramento as Crouch opened the scoring with a 10 yard field goal two and a half minutes into the half, then Oliphant scored his second touchdown of the game as he scored from 14 yards out. Crouch then added two more field goals, the first coming from 21 yards away and the next from 14 yards out. The final Gold Miners score came from the back ups as quarterback Kerwin Bell threw a 15-yard toss to slotback James Pruitt, making the final score 47-15, giving the Miners a much-needed win.

This game was the most impressive offensive showing of the season at home as Sacramento earned their third win of the season. Archer went 14 of 28 for 351 yards with one touchdown and no interceptions. The Miners had 583 combined yards, while their defense recorded three sacks and two interceptions while holding Ottawa's rushers to only 82 total yards.

Game Twelve (at Saskatchewan)

This game was a tale of two halves as the Roughriders took the lead when receiver Tre Everett caught a 12-yard pass from quarterback Kent Austin for the only score of the first quarter. Saskatchewan would add to their lead when kicker Dave Ridgway kicked a 30-yard field goal, and running back Mike Saunders scored from one yard away, followed by Ridgway's 10-yard field goal, making the score 20–0 at the half.

After the break, Archer got the Gold Miners on the board when he tossed a four yard pass to running back Troy Mills. Archer then threw his second touchdown as he connected with slotback Freeman Baysinger on an 83-yard touchdown strike. The Miners tied the game when kicker Crouch kicked two field goals, the first from 32 yards and the second a short 12-yarder. Saskatchewan answered as Austin led his team on an eight-play, 75-yard drive ending with his second touchdown pass, a 12-yard toss to slotback Jeff Fairholm, giving the Roughriders the lead and the win 27–20 in front of 25,367 hometown fans inside Taylor Field. Archer connected with eight different receivers in this game, as he went 23 of 37 for 298 yards with two touchdowns and no interceptions. He was also sacked three times, bringing his season total to 46.

Game Thirteen (Edmonton)

Coming into this game against the Eskimos, the Gold Miners were still in the playoff hunt despite their 3–9–0 record. A crowd of 15,914 were on hand to watch this game at Hornet's Field. Edmonton struck first as quarterback Damon Allen connected with receiver Trent Brown for a 58-yard touchdown pass. Archer then drove the Gold Miners 85 yards in five plays to even the score when he connected with receiver Titus Dixon for the nine-yard score, ending the quarter.

Edmonton's kicker Sean Fleming added a single when he missed a 49-yard field goal. Then Crouch added an 18-yard field goal to give Sacramento a 10–8 half time lead. This would be as close to winning as the Miners would get as Edmonton would come out fighting in the second half.

Eskimo kicker Fleming added a 45-yard field goal to open the scoring, then quarterback Allen would throw three second-half touchdowns. The first to Brown for his second touchdown, coming from 71 yards to cap a two-play drive of 74 yards. Next, Allen connected with Henry Gizmo Williams on a 37-yard pass for the touchdown. Sacramento answered as Crouch added a 22-yard kick, ending the quarter with Edmonton ahead 25–13.

In the final quarter, Allen and Brown connected for the third time with an 11-yard touchdown, giving the Eskimos a 19-point lead. Edmonton linebacker Wullie Pless closed the scoring when he sacked Archer in the end zone for the safety, giving the Eskimos a 34–13 win. With the loss, all hopes for the Miners to make the playoffs were gone. Damon Allen ripped the Gold Miners' defense as he threw for 482 yards and four touchdowns, as he went 24 of 32 passes and ran for 92 yards on 12 carries.

Archer, on the other hand, was hounded all game as he went 16 of 35 for 295 yards and one touchdown with one interception and was sacked four times, bringing the season total to 50.

Game Fourteen (at British Columbia)

As the Gold Miners entered the final month of their inaugural season and the final stretch of the pro football triathlon, they were still in search of their first road win in the CFL.

So on October 2nd, the Miners headed to British Columbia to play the Lions in front of 30,615 spectators at B.C. Place Stadium. The first score came just two minutes into the game as Lions cornerback Les Browne intercepted Archer and returned it 34 yards for the score. Lion kicker Lui Passaglia added two short field goals, the first from 19 yards away, then a 16-yarder giving B.C. a 13-point lead. Sacramento got on the board as Crouch got a single when he missed a 35 yard attempt, making the score 13–1 after one quarter in favor of the Lions.

Sacramento opened the second quarter scoring with a 31-yard field goal by Crouch, but B.C. answered with a 15-yard touchdown pass from quarterback Danny Barrett to receiver Lonnie Turner. The Gold Miners got their first touchdown with 13 seconds left in the half as Archer connected with receiver Joe Johnson from 17 yards away. The Lions started the second half scoring when Passaglia kicked a 40 field goal. Sacramento punter Pete Gardere added a single when his punt went into the end zone, making the score 23–12 with the Lions in front after three quarters.

Sacramento scored first roughly six minutes into the final quarter as Crouch missed a 43-yard field goal, earning the single. The other two scores came with less than a minute to play in the game as Archer threw his second touchdown to receiver Titus Dixon, cutting the Lions lead to 23–20. With just 43 seconds left in the game, perhaps the most memorable play of Sacramento's season happened as Crouch's onside kick was caught in mid-air by Gold Miner receiver James Pruitt, who returned it to the B.C. 20-yard line. Two plays later, Archer found Johnson for the winning score with a 26-yard touchdown pass. The catch would be Johnson's second of the game, giving the Miners their fourth win of the season and, more important, their first road win, a 27–23 come-from-behind victory. With this victory, Sacramento became the first "Non-Canadian" team to win a CFL game in Canada.

Archer finished the day completing 26 of 46 for 432 yards with three touchdowns and three interceptions. Archer was also sacked five times, bringing the season total to 55 in 14 games (not a record). Gold Miner defensive end Mark Ledbetter was named Defensive player of the week for his part in this win.

Game Fifteen (at Winnipeg)

The Gold Miners came into this game riding high after recording their first road victory in team history, hoping to make it two in a row. The Blue Bombers were in first place in the Eastern Division, having clinched the division title and a first-round bye. A crowd of 27,415 fans filled Winnipeg Stadium to watch the Gold Miners for the first time in Winnipeg.

Sacramento would score first as punter Pete Gardere got two singles off his first two punts, the first a 62-yard kick into the end zone, then a 57-yard boot into the end zone once again. The Blue Bombers scored as quarterback Matt Dunigan connected with receiver David Williams on a 15-yard score. Winnipeg kicker Troy Westwood would add two field goals, a 35-yarder and a 22-yard kick, making the score 13–2.

Then, just before the break, returner Joe Johnson returned the Blue Bomber punt 63 yards for the score. The first ever in Miner history, making the score 13–9 at the half with Winnipeg on top. Once again, Sacramento opened the second half scoring as Crouch connected on a 28-yard attempt, cutting the Bombers' lead to one 13–12. Winnipeg answered as Dunigan found Williams for a 32-yard touchdown. Archer then led Sacramento to the final score of the quarter when he connected with Titus Dixon from 20 yards away to pull the Miners within a point 20–19.

In the final quarter, the Blue Bombers put the game away with 13 straight points, starting with another field goal by Westwood from 18 yards away. Then Williams caught his third touchdown of the game, a 44-yard pass from backup Sam Garza. Finally, Westwood added his fourth field goal, a 27-yard kick, giving Winnipeg a 33–19 lead. The Miners then marched 89 yards in five plays to score when Archer connected with Dixon from 17 yards with 32 seconds left on the clock. Everyone on the Sacramento sideline was thinking would this be another onside kick miracle like the week before?? Winnipeg got the kick and held on for the win 32–26.

The Blue Bombers won the game but lost quarterback Matt Dunigan for the season with a torn Achilles heel. Yet Winnipeg would go on to play in the Grey Cup, losing to Calgary 24–10. Archer was sacked four times in this game, bringing the total to 59 in 15 games. He went 16 of 38 for 242 yards with two touchdowns and two interceptions.

Game Sixteen (Toronto)

The Gold Miners returned home to Hornet Field to play the Toronto Argonauts in front of 16,242 fans. Coming into this game, Toronto would have a chance to move into the final playoff spot in the east ahead of Ottawa, who had just lost their earlier game.

Toronto opened the scoring when quarterback Tracey Ham ran in from 21 yards away, and kicker Lance Chonyc missed a 52-yard attempt, earning the single. Sacramento then had a three-play drive going 67 yards, which ended with a 46-yard touchdown pass from Archer to receiver James Priutt as the quarter ended. Chonyc added another single, and Ham threw an 11-yard pass to running back Mike Clemons, making the score 16–7 in the visitor's favor. Ham and his teammates would watch in horror as to what was going to happen next.

Archer led the Gold Miners 85 yards in eight plays, ending with a 17-yard pass to receiver Rod Harris for the score. Archer then connected with receiver Joe Johnson on a 20-yard touchdown pass just before the half, putting the Gold Miners ahead 21–16. Sacramento would hold Toronto scoreless in the third quarter, while Crouch added a 30-yard field goal, and Archer scored his first rushing touchdown in CFL, a one-yard run to end the quarter.

Now up 31–16, the Miners scored again as Archer threw his fourth touchdown pass of the game, a seven-yard toss to Johnson, his second of the game. Trailing 38–16, Toronto's backup Quarterback Reggie Slack connected with receiver Manny Hazard, with Clemons running for the two-point convert to end the scoring. Sacramento earned their fifth win of the season as they won 38–24.

Archer threw for 489 yards, as he completed 29 of 43 passes with four touchdowns and no picks. Archer was sacked three times, making the season total 62 sacks (still not a CFL record). With the win, the Gold Miners again broke the franchise single-game record for the most offensive yards in a single game with 541 total yards.

Game Seventeen (at Calgary)

Sacramento headed to Calgary to play the Stampeders in front of 26,015 fans at McMahon Stadium. The Gold Miners were looking for their sixth win of the season and their third in four games. Calgary started the scoring on the opening kickoff as kicker Matt Mclaughlin booted a 93-yard kick, which sailed into the end zone, earning him a single. This would be a sign of things to come for Sacramento.

Just past the six-minute mark of the quarter, Calgary quarterback Doug Flutie connected with receiver Will Moore for a 19-yard touchdown. Sacramento would get on the board when punter Gardere nailed a 91-yard kick into the end zone for the single. Flutie then answered with a 33-yard pass to slotback Dave Sapunjis for the score, putting the Stampeders ahead 22–1. Calgary would score again as backup Steve Taylor ran in from one yard out. The Gold Miners would score with less than a minute to play in the half as Archer tossed a one-yard pass to running back Mike Pringle, making the half time score 22–8 in Calgary's favor. As the second half got under way, the Gold Miners were hoping to make a comeback, yet Calgary's Mclaughlin did all the third quarter scoring as he kicked two field goals, one from 27 and then from 33 yards. The Gold Miners would be shut out the entire second half while the Stampeders continued to score as Taylor threw a 10-yard pass to Moore, his second of the game. Mclaughlin would kick his third and fourth field goals of the game, one from 24 yards and then from 21 yards, to close out the scoring, giving the Stampeders a 41–8 lopsided win over Sacramento. Mark Mclaughlin was the game's leading scorer with 17 points from four field goals, four converts and a single.

With his touchdown catch, Calgary receiver Dave Sapunjis became the FIRST Canadian-born player to have 100 or more receptions in a season.

This loss shocked the Miners, who, coming into this game, had scored 91 points in their last three games, two wins and a loss. Archer was sacked three times as he threw for 191 yards while completing 20 of 35 passes for one touchdown and no picks.

Game Eighteen (British Columbia)

Heading into their final game of the season Sacramento was hosting British Columbia at Hornet Field with 18,748 fans in attendance, the second largest all season. The Gold Miners had something to prove, and they proved it. Following the lopsided loss last game, Archer and his team had a chip on their shoulders. Looking to prove they were for real, the Miners beat up the Lions as they scored the first three touchdowns and never looked back.

To start things off, running back Mike Oliphant ran in from six yards out, then back Mike Pringle scored on a one-play 44-yard run. Not to be outdone, Archer scored on a one-yard run.

B.C. got on the board just as the quarter ended when kicker Lui Passaglia kicked a 26-yard field goal. Crouch then added a single when he missed a 43-yard attempt. Passaglia added a 37-yard kick to give the Lions six points. Archer then threw the first of his four touchdowns, a 20-yard toss to receiver Carl Parker to make the score 29–6 at the half.

To begin the second half, the Gold Miners' defense got into the act as defensive end Greg Joelson recovered a B.C. fumble and raced 31 yards for the score. The Lions lost three fumbles in this game. About six minutes later, Archer threw his second touchdown, a 13-yard strike to receiver Tre Everett. The Lions finally got a touchdown when quarterback Danny McManus connected with receiver Ray Alexander from 22 yards out. Sacramento receiver Carl Parker caught the first of his two touchdowns as Archer hit him from three yards away. McManus then led his team on a six-play 58-yard drive capped off with a one-yard pass to receiver Darren Flutie, making the score

50–20 after three quarters with Sacramento leading.

Archer connected with Parker once again on a two yard toss for Parker's second score of the game. Then Pringle would run one in from three yards for his second score. The Lions would add one more score before this nightmare would end, as running back Sam Millington scored from one yard out. Sacramento won this game 64–27 to prove they were for real, and the 64 points scored would be the most by one team during the 1993 season.

Mike Oliphant's lone reception, which covered 83 yards, was enough to help him capture the league's yards from scrimmage title. Titus Dixon had three catches for 88 yards helping him to exceed 1,000 yards receiving on the season. Archer became only the third quarterback in league history to pass for more than 6,000 yards (6,023) in a single season. (Doug Flutie, 1991, B.C., 6,619 yards and Kent Austin, 1992, Sask., 6,225 yards)

In this game, Archer went 17 of 28 for 375 yards and four touchdowns with one interception. He was also sacked three times bringing the season total to 68 sacks, still not a record.(1986, Toronto, 103 sacks and 1988, Ottawa, 82 sacks are the records.)

The performances of defensive back Bobby Humphery, defensive lineman Mark Ledbetter and David Archer earned them the league's player of the week awards. Humphrey was voted Defensive player, as he had five tackles, one interception, and one tackle on special teams. Ledbetter was voted Defensive Lineman (his second time; week 14 was his other), and Archer was voted Offensive player of the week.

Running back Mike Oliphant and wide receiver Rod Harris were voted to the West All-Star team, while kicker Jim Crouch scored 156 points, placing him in fifth among first-year players for scoring. He also tied a record for the most converts in a game with nine, which he made in the last game.

Punter Pete Gardere was the West's punting average leader with a 42.2 average. David Archer captured the record for the most passes thrown with 701, plus most passes completed with 406 and passing yardage with 6,023 yards. The 64 points would be the second-highest score in the three-year history of the U.S. teams. The Gold Miners set the record for the most wins by an expansion team with six wins.

Let's play a little game now. If the CFL was just one division instead of two the Gold Miners would have made the playoffs. Let's see why. Take a look at the would-be standings:

Calgary.......15–3–0

Winnipeg......14–4–0

Edmonton 12–6–0

Saskatchewan.....11–7–0

B. C. 10–8–0

Sacramento....6–12–0

Hamilton.......6–12–0

Ottawa....... 4–14–0

Toronto........3–15–0

Based on the points, Sacramento had 498 points while Hamilton had 316 points, so the Miners had 182 more points than the Tiger-cats. Then, based on the two-game series (which the CFL likes to use to decide the tie-breakers), each team won a game and lost a game, yet Sacramento out scored Hamilton 60–40 in the two-game series, which would have earned them the final playoff spot. The Gold Miners would have played Edmonton in the first round in Edmonton. Sacramento would have lost to the Eskimos based on the regular season games, as the Eskimos won all three games.

Final note: Of the Miners' 12 losses, nine of them were by nine points or less, plus they only lost three games in a row, twice during the regular season (games 1–3 and 8–10), and they won four of their last nine games.

CFL '94

With the Triathlon over, it was time to get ready for the 1994 season with three new teams from the states. First, there was the Las Vegas Posse who were owned by Nick Mileti out of Cleveland, Ohio. Mileti was the former owner of the NBA's Cleveland Cavaliers, the MLB's Indians (now the Guardians), and the NHL's Cleveland Barons. He also purchased the Cleveland Arena and founded the Cleveland Crusaders of the WHL. The Posse played at Sam Boyd Stadium in Whitney, NV (a suburb of Las Vegas). Next, there was the Shreveport Pirates who were owned by Bernard Glieberman and his son Lonnie. Now, the Gliebermans were the former owners of the Ottawa Rough Riders, and they wanted to move the team to Shreveport, but the league rejected the move, so the Glibermans sold the Roughriders to Bruce Firestone and used the money to attain the Shreveport team. The Pirates played at Independence Stadium in Shreveport. Finally, there was the Baltimore "CFL" Colts who were owned by Jim Speros, who made his money in the real estate business. Baltimore played their home games in the famed Memorial Stadium, where the NFL Colts played.

As the season began the Gold Miners made the record books yet again as they became the first U.S. city to host an "official" CFL regular season game between two American teams as Sacramento hosted Las Vegas. This game was played at Hornet Stadium on July 8, 1994, with 14,816 fans on hand to see the Posse defeat the Miners 32–26. Meanwhile, in Toronto, the Argos lost to Baltimore 28–20, while Shreveport lost to Ottawa 40–10 in Ottawa. (This would be the second straight season Ottawa opened the season at home against one of the U.S. teams, as they hosted Sacramento in 1993.) Archer would finish the first game going 24 of 36 for 336 yards with three touchdowns and three interceptions while suffering two sacks.

After this game, the Miners went on the road for the next two games, with the first stop being in Hamilton against the Tiger-cats. Sacramento came out on top, winning 25–22 in front of 19,291 fans in attendance. The next game was in Las Vegas and a rematch with the Posse. Sacramento won the game 22–20, as just 10,740 fans were in attendance. David Archer finished these two games going 37 of 68 for 667 yards with four touchdowns and three interceptions while being sacked 12 times, 10 of those coming in the game against the Posse.

Game four saw the Gold Miners at home to face Saskatchewan with 14,828 spectators in attendance. This crowd witnessed a very close game as the home town Miners edged the Roughriders 30–27 to improve to 3-1-0. Sacramento receiver Rod Harris was named Offensive Player of the Week as he caught four passes for 87 yards. One was for a 32 touchdown, and he also added a 102-yard punt return. Archer went 15 of 34 for 310 yards with three touchdowns and zero interceptions.

The next two games were on the road, with the first stop in B.C. against the Lions, with 18,459 spectators on hand to witness the Lions defeat the Miners 46-10. This game was the start of a four game losing streak for Sacramento. Up next was the game in Calgary against the Stampeders as 21,110 fans were in attendance to watch as their hometown club defeated the visitors 25–11 to even the Gold Miners record at 3–3–0. Archer would complete 42 of 78 passes for 597 yards with just one touchdown and four interceptions. Archer was sacked 10 times in these two games for a total of 26 sacks in only six games. But the bad news for Sacramento was that Archer injured his finger and would miss the next game.

Game seven saw the Miners hosting Edmonton without David Archer. The crowd of 13,959 fans were ready to see how Kerwin Bell would play in Archer's place. Bell, if you remember, was the Orlando Thunder's quarterback in World Bowl '92 against the Surge. Bell would finish 28 of 46 for 312 yards with no touchdowns and one interception, while Bell was sacked five times as the Eskimos defeated Sacramento 44–15. The following game was in Winnipeg against the Blue Bombers, as 21,804 fans witnessed the return of David Archer. Winnipeg would go on to win in a very close game, 30–27, as Archer went 21 of 44 for 385 yards with three touchdowns and two interceptions while being sacked twice. With this loss, the Gold Miners losing streak reached four games. As the Miners headed home to host B.C., Sacramento would enter the record books once more as they played B.C. at Hornet Field in front of 12,633 fans in attendance. The reason these two teams made the record books was that they battled to a tie with 15 points apiece. This would be the ONLY tie in the three-year history of the American teams. Now, at the midway point of the season, Sacramento's record was 3–5–1, and Archer's stats were 157 of 314 for 2,567 yards with 15 touchdowns and 13 interceptions, being sacked 31 times. Kerwin Bell went 28 of 48 for 312 yards with zero touchdowns, one interception, and being sacked five times.

To start the second half of the season, the Miners would travel east to Baltimore to play the CFLers, as they were now called, after losing the lawsuit to the NFL and the Colts. This game was played in front of a record crowd of 42,116 fans who packed Baltimore's Memorial Stadium. Sacramento went on to win this game 30–29 as Archer had a good game, going 22 of 38 for 277 yards with three touchdowns and two interceptions while being sacked twice.

Up next, the Gold Miners played host to Calgary in front of 17,192 spectators who watched as Archer left the game with a dislocated finger injury that would end his season. Archer went five of six for 73 yards before his injury. Kerwin Bell played a good game, going 16 of 32 for 196 yards with one touchdown and two interceptions, being sacked twice, but Sacramento still lost 39–25 in front of the largest home crowd all season.

Sacramento would travel to Saskatchewan to play the Roughriders in front of 23,669 fans who watched as Bell got his first start of the season and of his CFL career. Bell would help lead the Miners to a 19–16 victory over the home team as he went 13 of 25 for 129 yards with no touchdowns and one interception before he left the game, giving way to Jimmy Kemp, son of Bills' great quarterback Jack Kemp. Kemp went five of ten for 54 yards with no touchdowns or interceptions. Yet the real hero of this game was kicker Roman Anderson, who scored all the Miners 19 points as he kicked six field goals and one single and was named Offensive Player of the Week.

Game 14 saw the Miners hosting Toronto with 13,050 fans inside Hornet Field. These faithful fans watched as Sacramento edged the Argos 34–32 to move one game above .500 at 7–6–1 with a shot at the playoffs still in sight. Bell finished 20 of 33 for 339 yards with two touchdowns and one interception while being sacked twice. Up next was a game against the Pirates in Shreveport who were still looking for their first win in team history. Bell had a bad day as he finished 14 of 39 for217 yards with no touchdowns, interceptions or sacks, as the Miners fell to the Pirates 24-12, giving Shreveport their first win of the season and giving Sacramento the honor of being the first team to lose to the Pirates.

After this disappointing loss Sacramento returned home to host Ottawa in front of 13,760 fans who watched as the Miners routed the Rough Riders 44–9 as Bell went 15 of 23 for 254 yards with two touchdowns and one interception while getting sacked just once. Now at 8–7–1, Sacramento was still very much alive in the playoff race.

Sacramento headed to Edmonton for their final road game of the season with a crowd of 29,322 loyal fans in attendance. The Eskimos defeated the Gold Miners 22–16 as Bell went 17 of 33 for 206 yards, with one touchdown, interception, and one sack. On the season so far the Gold Miners gave up 47 sacks in 17 games.

The final regular season game had Sacramento hosting Baltimore, with Sacramento hoping for a playoff spot while the CFLers were already in with a 12–5–0 record after defeating Winnipeg 57–10 to earn a tie for the division title (the CFLers' 12 wins would become a new record for an expansion team, breaking the old record set by Sacramento a year ago with six wins). Once more, the Gold Miners made up for their loss the week before as the crowd of 14,056 watched as Sacramento held the visitors scoreless, winning 18–0 to earn the only shutout in the three-year history of the American clubs. Kerwin Bell went 11 of 22 for 77 yards with zero touchdowns, interceptions, and no sacks. The Miners also earned the only back-to-back safeties in this game. The first came when Baltimore punter Jeff Miller stepped out of the end zone. Then, on Baltimore's next series, backup quarterback John Congemi fumbled, and the ball rolled into the end zone as Congemi recovered, but he was ruled down by contact. Sacramento running back Troy Mills was named Offensive Player of the Week as he ran for 181 yards on 33 carries with one touchdown in the game.

KEY NOTES FOR THE 1994 SEASON:

- First U.S. city to host an official CFL game between two U.S. cities when, on July 8, 1994, Sacramento lost to the Las Vegas Posse 32–26 in Sacramento.

- Played in the ONLY tie game in the three-year history of the American teams when, on September 2, 1994, the Gold Miners tied the B.C. Lions at 15 apiece.

- Played before a record crowd of 42,116 fans in Baltimore's Memorial Stadium, defeating the CFLers 30–29 on October 10, 1994.

- First team to lose to the Shreveport Pirates 24–12 on October 16, 1994, at Independence Stadium in Shreveport (the Pirates were 0-14-0 before the game).

- Quarterback David Archer would miss the last six games and seven altogether with a dislocated finger.

- Played their last game in Sacramento on November 5, 1994, an 18–0 victory over Baltimore, which included the first back-to-back safeties in the history of the U.S. teams.

- Sacramento had three players named Offensive Players of the Week:

  - Week three: wide receiver Rod Harris as he had two touchdowns and 85 yards receiving. Harris was also named to the CFL All-Star team in 1994.

  - Week 13: Kicker Roman Anderson as he scored all 19 of the Gold Miners' points in a 19–16 victory over Saskatchewan.

  - Week 18: running back Troy Mills as he ran for 181 yards with one touchdown on 33 carries in the 18–0 win over Baltimore.

- Baltimore would become the first U.S. city to host a CFL playoff game when they defeated Toronto 34–15 en route to becoming the first American team to play for the Grey Cup, losing 26–23 on a late B.C. field goal.

CFL '95

The 1995 CFL season saw many changes and one big change, first Las Vegas was gone after two attempts to move the team. Next two new teams were added, the Birmingham Barracudas, owned by Fred Smith, founder of FedEx company, playing their home games inside the famed Legion Field and the Memphis Mad Dogs, owned by Arthur Williams Jr., founder of Primerica Financial Services, and playing their home games at the Liberty Bowl, making the total number of teams south of the border at five. Baltimore finally had a nickname, "the Stallions," who were looking to return to the Grey Cup after losing last year's game to B.C. Then Sacramento moved to San Antonio, becoming the only U.S. team to have a regulation-size CFL field inside the Alamodome.

With all these changes, the biggest one was that for the first time in the league's history, there would be no East or West Divisions as they were replaced with North and South Divisions. In the north were all the Canadian teams, while in the south were the five U.S. teams. The playoff format would be the top three clubs from the south would qualify for the postseason, and in the north, the top five teams would qualify with the fifth team (Winnipeg in this case) would play the top team in the south.

San Antonio would play their first three games against division opponents, starting with a road game against the Pirates in Shreveport as 15,133 fans saw the Texans defeat the home team 47-24 as Archer went 19 of 26 for229 yards with two touchdowns and no interceptions. He also ran for a touchdown from a yard out.

The Texans then headed to Baltimore to play the Stallions as 31,016 spectators witnessed the Stallions score 50 points en route to a 50-24 victory. In this game, both teams combined for eight sacks, four apiece. Archer finished completing 21 of 38 passes for 348 yards with two touchdowns and one interception.

Next San Antonio headed home for their first game inside the Alamodome against Baltimore in a home-and-home series. With 18,112 spectators on hand to see the Stallions defeat the Texans 28-23, Archer went 24 of 38 for 334 yards with one touchdown and no interception. San Antonio then hosted the Eskimos before a crowd of 12,856 fans who watched their team defeat Edmonton 32-27 to even their record at 2-2-0. Quarterback David Archer went 23 of 36 for 298 yards with one touchdown and two interceptions. Archer also ran for a one-yard score before he suffered a hamstring injury in this game, which kept him out of almost four games as he would miss game five in Winnipeg while playing one quarter in Saskatchewan before being replaced by Jim Kemp.

Their next two games saw the Texans on the road, with their first stop in Winnipeg as 20,961 watched as the Blue Bombers would edge San Antonio 20-17. Kemp went 13 of 28 for 194 yards, with no touchdowns and four interceptions. Four days later, the Texans were in Regina to play the Saskatchewan Roughriders, with a crowd of 22,215 fans who saw San Antonio defeat Saskatchewan 36-15. Texans kicker Roman Anderson scored 18 points to help win this game, as Archer went 6 of 10 for 130 yards while Kemp completed just one pass for a seven-yard score to receiver Mike Saunders.

The Texans would return home to play Memphis for the first time, with a crowd of 15,557 in attendance who saw San Antonio hold the Mad Dogs to only nine points, winning 24-9. The Texans' record was now 4-3-0 after winning two straight games, with Kemp completing 11 of 18 passes for 174 yards with two scores and two picks.

Their eighth game of the season had the Texans hosting Calgary in front of the largest crowd of the season, as 22,043 fans were in the stands. The Stampeders would hold on to win this game 38-32, as

Kemp went 21 of 32 for 234 yards for one score and no picks.

San Antonio then would travel to Hamilton to take on the Tiger-cats with 20,520 fans in attendance to see the Texans drop a four-point game to Hamilton 35-31 to reach the midway point of the season with a 4-5-0 and a two-game losing streak and two games out of first place. In his first game back, Archer went 13 of 31 for 302 yards with one touchdown and one pick.

As the second half of the season got started, the Texans were still hoping for a postseason berth as they would travel to Memphis to play at the Liberty Bowl, home of the Mad Dogs. A crowd of 16,223 spectators were on hand to witness as the visitors held the Mad Dogs to just six points, losing 26-6. Archer went 19 of 28 for 258 yards and no scores with two interceptions. The win gave the Texans a push for the postseason as this was the start of a five-game winning streak that saw San Antonio outscored their opponents 184–75 with the first game in Toronto's Skydome for their game against the Argonauts with just 14,593 fans in attendance. San Antonio would win this game by a 48-27 score. Archer would have a great game, going 19 of 32 for 383 yards and three scores with one interception.

For their next game, the Texans returned home to play Toronto in another home-and-home series as the crowd of 16,028 fans watched San Antonio defeat the Argos 42-21. Archer threw for two scores while going 16 of 25 for 250 yards and no picks.

Hamilton was the next opponent that San Antonio would face at home with 14,593 spectators in attendance to witness as San Antonio won this match by a lopsided score of 45-7. David Archer finished 17 of 31 for 186 yards with two touchdowns and one interception.

For their 14th game of the season, the Texans would travel to Ottawa to play the Rough Riders at Lansdowne Park, as 19,957 fans were in the stands. Once again, the Texans won another lopsided game 49-14 to improve their record to 9-5-0, just behind Baltimore in the South Division. Once again, Archer went 21 of 33 for 345 yards with four touchdowns and just one interception.

Entering the final month of games, San Antonio would travel to Birmingham to play the Barracudas at the famed Legion Field. One of the smallest crowds to see a CFL game was on hand as the 6,859 fans watched as the Barracudas ended the Texans win streak at five games with a 38-28 victory. Once again Archer threw for over 300 yards as he went 23 of 40 for 340 yards, with just one touchdown and no picks (this would be the Texans' lone defeat during the second half of the season). San Antonio would finish the season at home with their first opponent being Ottawa, as 10,027 fans watched as their home team defeated the Rough Riders 43-30. Archer would throw four touchdowns while finishing 19 of 29 for 288 yards and no picks.

Up next would be Shreveport, who had just won their fifth game of the season the week before as they defeated the Tiger-cats 26-14. With a crowd of 14,437 on hand to see the Texans defeat the Pirates 35-26 to lock up second place in the South Division, two games behind the Stallions who had already won the Division. Archer again passed for over 300 yards, going 20 of 29 for 346 yards with four touchdowns and one interception.

The final game of the regular season had the Texans hosting the Barracudas in front of 19,025 spectators, which saw a tough game with San Antonio holding on the win 48-42 to finish the season at 12-6-0, three games behind Baltimore, who finished at 15-3-0. Archer went 21-32 for 427 yards and two scores with no interceptions.

In the South Division semi-final games, Baltimore hosted the Winnipeg Blue Bombers, who were the fifth team in the North, while San Antonio hosted Birmingham for the second straight week. In this game, the Texans left nothing to chance as they won this game 52-9, scoring the third most points in playoff history. Archer opened the scoring for the Texans on a one-yard run before throwing three touchdown passes of 74, 38, and 5 yards, finishing the game with 14 of 24 for 309 yards with the three scores and no interceptions. Little did the crowd of only 13,031 spectators know that they were watching the last CFL game in San Antonio. As the Stallions defeated Winnipeg 36-21, earning the right to host the Texans in the South Final.

So, in what would be the LAST CFL game in the States, the Stallions would defeat the Texans 21-11 for the right to play in the Grey Cup. This game was not as close as the score makes it look, as the Texans trailed 15–1 at the half and 21–1 late in the third quarter. Yet there were no fumbles or interceptions in this game, and just one touchdown…it was the final score of the game coming at the 12:49 mark of the fourth quarter. Archer connected with receiver Mark Stock for a two-yard touchdown. (It is odd that the last touchdown scored during the last game on U.S. soil came in the last quarter.) Archer finished the game going 24 of 45 for 245 yards with one touchdown and no interceptions.

On November 19, 1995, the 83rd Grey Cup was played as 52,064 spectators witnessed CFL history as the Baltimore Stallions defeated the Calgary Stampeders 37-20 to become the ONLY non-Canadian team to hoist the Grey Cup. But for the Stallions, there would be no repeat, no celebration…EVER, as the league went back to an All-Canadian league in 1996, as Baltimore would move to Montreal.

KEYNOTES:

- San Antonio would be the only U.S. city to have a regulation size CFL field.

- The Texans five game win streak would be the longest of the team's three year history.

- The 52 points San Antonio scored in the playoff game against Birmingham would be the most scored in the postseason during the three-year U.S. teams and third most all-time.

- Fred Anderson's club would finish their three-year run with 27 wins,26 losses, and one tie, plus one win and one loss in the postseason.

- The Texans had four members named to the Players of the Week. First, in week four, Guard Chuck Esty was named Lineman of the Week, while wide receiver Joe Kralik was named Offensive Player as he had 13 catches for 200 yards and one touchdown.

- In week five, running back Mike Saunders was named Offensive player as he ran for 70 yards on 12 carries.

- Week nine linebacker David Harper was named Defensive player for his play against Hamilton.

- Harper and Saunders were named to the CFL Southern All-Star Team, along with center Mike Kiselak and kicker Roman Anderson who finished with 235 total points.

- The lone touchdown scored by San Antonio in the South final against Baltimore would be the "LAST" touchdown of the CFL on U.S. soil.

- As stated before, the '95 season would be the final season for the American clubs.

- As for Fred Anderson, the owner of both the Surge and Gold Miners and whose company built the Arco Arena, giving him a major role in the Triathlon, he was honored in 1998 when he was named to the Sacramento Hall Of Fame. Also, in 2007, he was honored by Sacramento State College when they named the field at Hornet Stadium in his honor. Yet as of the writing of this book neither Fred Anderson nor David Archer are in the Pro Football Hall of Fame or the CFL Hall of Fame for their part in the Pro Football Triathlon.

In Conclusion

After the 1995 season ended with the Stallions becoming the first and only American team to win the Grey Cup, things started to fall apart quickly. Shreveport left for Norfolk, VA, without the league's approval or without any stadium, just an office in Norfolk. Memphis folded, Birmingham tried to find a home in Shreveport, but in the end, they folded as well. Baltimore was a champion without a home as they were looking into moving to Houston, TX, or Jackson, Miss., after the Browns announced their move to Baltimore in 1995, but again, they too could not find a place to play, so Spenos headed to Montreal and became the new Alouettes. Once more, Anderson found himself the sole American team, and he decided enough was enough and called it quits, putting the final nail in the U.S. coffin and ending the CFL experiment's three-year run. CFL football in the States was over, and almost in Canada as well. The CFL would need a three million dollar loan from the NFL just to stay afloat, which the CFL did pay back.

In 1994, when the Gold Miners left for San Antonio, it left the River City without a pro football team again, but it did have the 1992 World Bowl title and the title of "Pro Football's Triathlon City" as they played in three different leagues with three different styles of play in less than a year (see the diagrams). If you think this feat was easy, consider everything that had to happen to have this event reach completion. If the Denver Dynamite never moved to Los Angeles, then almost being sued by the Wings bike club, and moved to Sacramento, also if the NFL decided to play the 1993 WLAF season, the Surge would have been there instead of in the CFL for the '93 season as the Gold Miners, to make Sacramento "Pro Football's Triathlon City."

Let's look at how this feat reached the football world. In the

WLAF, the city of Sacramento reached two continents, North America and Europe, five countries, England, France, Germany, Canada, and the United States, five states and one province: California, Alabama, Ohio, Texas, Florida, and Quebec, nine cities: London, Barcelona, Frankfurt, Montreal, Columbus, Birmingham, San Antonio, Orlando, and Sacramento.

In the Arena League, the city reached:

One country, the United States, eight states: Arizona, Michigan, New York, Ohio, Louisiana, Florida, Texas, and California, twelve cities: Albany, Charlotte, Cincinnati, Cleveland, Dallas, Detroit, Orlando, Phoenix, Sacramento, San Antonio, and Tampa Bay.

In the CFL, the city reached:

Two countries, Canada and the U.S., five provinces and one State: Alberta, Ontario, British Columbia, Manitoba, Saskatchewan, and California, nine cities, Winnipeg, Toronto, Hamilton, Regina, Ottawa, Calgary, Vancouver, Edmonton, and Sacramento.

In addition to these places, Fred Anderson's Club also reached Raleigh/Durham, N.C. Meadowlands, NJ. Baltimore, MD, Memphis, Tenn., Las Vegas, NV, and Shreveport, LA, during their seasons (1991, 1994, 1995).

Pro Football would return to Sacramento in 2010 after 15 years (1995-2010) when the United Football League moved the California Redwoods to the River City after poor attendance in both San Francisco and San Jose forced the move to Sacramento. The Redwoods would lose their name following a name the team contest with the team being called the Sacramento Mountain Lions, with NFL coach Dennis Green returning as head coach.

The UFL's 2009 season saw the Las Vegas Locomotives play the Florida Tuskers for the title, with Las Vegas defeating previous unbeaten Florida 20-17 in overtime. In 2010 Vegas and Florida returned while California moved to Sacramento and New York to Hartford, with Omaha being added.

In their first game, Sacramento faced Hartford in Hartford, with the Colonials winning 27-10 with 14,384 in attendance. Their next game was at Hornet Stadium, with over 20,000 fans in attendance to watch as the Mountain Lions defeated Florida 24-20 to hand the Tuskers their "first regular season loss." Sacramento would lose the next two games, first to the Nighthawks in Omaha 20-17 with 23,416 on hand. Then at home with 19,000 fans watching as Las Vegas won 26-3, holding Sacramento to their lowest point total ever. The Mountain Lions then traveled to Orlando to play the Tuskers at the Citrus Bowl with 10,066 fans watching as Sacramento won the game 21-17. Again, Sacramento dropped the next two games 27-26 to Hartford as 13,500 spectators watched this defeat. Next was a 27-24 loss to Las Vegas as 13,622 fans battled the Nevada heat to watch the Locos win. For their final game of 2010, Sacramento hosted the Nighthawks with 20,000 fans who watched as their team dominated Omaha 41-3 to even their record at 4-4-0, as Sacramento set a record for the largest margin of victory at 38 points.

In 2011, the league saw Hartford fold and the Tuskers leave Florida for Virginia, changing their nickname to the Destroyers. The Mountain Lions started the season with a three-game losing streak, losing first to Las Vegas 23-17 at Hornet Stadium with 19,938 spectators in attendance. Next, the Mountain Lions hosted Omaha, with 17,612 spectators in attendance to see the visitors defeat the Mountain Lions 33-30. For their third game of the season, Sacramento headed to the Virginia Beach Sportsplex to play the Destroyers with only 12,617 fans in attendance as Virginia won in a lopsided game 28-6 for the first game of a home and home series with the Destroyers. In what would be the final game at Hornet Stadium, a crowd of 18,794 spectators watched as the Mountain Lions would defeat the unbeaten Destroyers 27-20 in the "only" overtime regular season game. After this game, the league would cancel the rest of the season and have Las Vegas play the Destroyers in Virginia for the title. The Destroyers would hold Vegas to only three points to win the FINAL championship game 17-3 with a crowd of 14,172 spectators at the Virginia Beach Sportsplex.

The league also had the Nighthawks playing the Mountain Lions in Omaha in what was called the Consolation Game, with the winner being awarded third place as both teams were 1-3-0. A crowd of 10,123 fans were on hand to see as Sacramento would score with 2:39 left on the clock to force overtime, with the game tied at 19. Sacramento's running back Cory Ross would score his second touchdown from 23 yards away to give the visitors a 25-19 overtime win. In case you are not keeping track, this win was the Mountain Lions' second straight overtime victory. (This is an extra bonus fact: from 1960 to 1970, the NFL played a consolation game following each season as the two second-place teams, one from each division, would play in this game, also called the "playoff" game. Many great teams played in these games, the Colts, Packers, Cowboys, and more, but after the merger the league did away with this game.) (see chart)

The 2012 season started with the Mountain Lions' move from Hornet Stadium to Raley Field to help cut costs. Raley was an old Minor League Baseball park with little seating inside. There were no changes as all four clubs from the 2011 season returned, Las Vegas, Omaha, Sacramento and Virginia the defending champs. The Mountain Lions opened the season at home against Omaha with just 8,023 fans on hand as the Nighthawks defeated Sacramento 24-20. For their next game, the Mountain Lions would play in Virginia Beach against the Destroyers, with only 5,316 spectators in attendance. Virginia went on to defeat Sacramento 37-29 setting a record for the most combined points scored as both clubs scored 66 points. In what would be the LAST pro football game in the River City, the 5,210 fans watched as the Locos handed their home team a 20-9 defeat.

Sacramento would play their last pro game in the Virginia Beach Sportsplex against the Destroyers with no account of just how many spectators were in the stands. One thing is for sure: the ones who were there saw the Mountain Lions earn their only win of the season, a 20-17 victory.

After the game, the league suspended the rest of the season, stating to return in the spring of 2013; this would never happen. This league, just like other leagues, would drown in a sea of debt as many players were paid $1,000 instead of the contracted $3,500 per game. Here is a fun fact: Las Vegas played all four years or seasons, totalling 25 games (22 regular and 3 title games), while the Baltimore Stallions of the CFL played 23 games in 1995 (2 preseason, 18 regular and 3 postseason). This shows just how much trouble the UFL was really having!

Notes and Records:

- 2011– Special teams player of the year Aaron Woods kick returner Sacramento.

- Played in the only consolation game in Omaha, a 25-19 overtime win.

- First win; week two, 2010, at Florida. Sacramento 24 - Florida 20.

- Last win: week four, 2012, at Virginia. Sacramento 20 - Virginia 17.

- Most points scored by one team in a game: 41. Three teams: 2010, Sacramento, week 9 against Omaha 41-3 win; 2010, Florida, week 9 against Hartford 41-7 win; 2012, Las Vegas, week 2 against Omaha 41-6 win; 2009, L.V., week 5, against New York 41-10 win; 2009, L.V., week 7 against New York 41-7 win.

- Most points combined both teams: 66 points, Virginia - 37 and Sacramento – 29, week 2, 2012.

- Largest margin of victory: 38 points, 2010, week 9, Sacramento (41) Omaha (3).

- Fewest points allowed in a game: 3 points, 2010, week 9, Sacramento versus Omaha 41-3 win.

- Smallest margin of victory: 1 point, 2010, week 7, Hartford at Sacramento, 27-26 win.

- Played in two of the three overtime games in league history, winning both games.

Author Ron Snyder wrote in his book "The Baltimore Stallions" on page 145, quoting tackle Shar Pourdanesh, saying that "The Stallions were the product of a perfect storm and perfect timing. Had Baltimore NOT lost out on expansion, we never would have been there. Had the World League not folded, we likely would not have been there. Had the strike not occurred in baseball, we likely would not have gotten as much media attention as we did. I'm not sure the Stallions would have worked in any other time, but that one."

Closing comment. Once again we need to consider all the events that took place for this historic triathlon to happen and happen without any planning. To have these events happen as they did would be like sitting in a park and seeing a leprechaun riding a unicorn handing out three-dollar bills! This was a very rare event that just happened to have all the pieces fall into place at just the right time and place, with the right people to see this event to the finish line. It is important to keep in mind that the city of Sacramento can forever be called "PRO FOOTBALL'S FIRST TRIATHLON CITY!"

Final Thoughts

It seems to me from stories I have read that the CFL is trying to forget or bury the time when the American teams were part of their league. Why do I say this? Reason one: When the Stallions left Baltimore and relocated to Montreal and were renamed the Alouettes, for the first few years, their media guides listed the Alouettes as getting their roots from Baltimore, but then the league changed the team's origin as a rebirth of the old Alouettes. The original Alouettes folded in 1987.

Reason two: The CFL Hall of Fame has very little about one of the greatest time periods in their history (my opinion). In 1995, the league had 13 teams, the most in their history. They had two new divisions (North and South), which were brand new. The display they had when I was there was a small 4x8 or so shadow box type display. Reason three: From the games I have watched, there is no mention of the seven former teams from the States. Yet I understand the reason why so many CFL fans may want to forget this time frame, but let me make this point. I am a Buffalo Bills fan and have to live with the Four Super Bowl losses and the current playoff defeats mainly to the Chiefs.

What the CFL did in that three-year span was only done by three other leagues in pro football's first century, and the NFL was NOT one of them! These three were the All-American Football Conference, which ran from 1946 to 1949 with eight teams in their first three years and seven in the final season when Brooklyn and New York merged. During the four years, the league saw one team fold (Miami Seahawks, no ties to Seattle) and two teams change nicknames (Buffalo Bisons to Bills and Chicago Rockets to Hornets).

Next up is the fourth American Football League which ran from

1960 to 1970 and started with eight teams for the first six seasons. During these first six years, the league overcame many struggles to survive. Two teams had to move: the Chargers from Los Angeles to San Diego and the Dallas Texans to Kansas City. Two other teams needed a bailout from Buffalo owner Ralph Wilson to stay afloat (Oakland and N.Y. Jets). By 1968, two new teams were added, Miami and Cincinnati, and in 1970, this league merged with the NFL and is now the current AFC.

The final one is the United States Football League, which ran from 1983 to 1985. This league was the first spring league which started with 12 teams in 1983 growing to 18 teams in 1984 before dropping down to 14 in 1985. Then, in 1986 moved to a fall schedule before suspending operations only to fold in the summer. There were eight teams that wanted to play in the '86 season, yet it never came to be.

We now see that these leagues had to overcome many, many problems just to continue operations, so why did the CFL really pull the plug on the U.S. expansion? We may never really know why, but it may be that the Stallions had played in two Grey Cups in two seasons, winning the cup in 1995 and sending the Grey Cup south. CFL fans did not want the Grey Cup trophy to be just like the Stanley Cup, going back and forth across the border!! Football fans in Canada wanted their game to remain "THEIR" game and not become another trophy passed between two countries. So, in my opinion, this is why CFL leaders and fans want to forget the U.S. expansion.

Notes

Chapter One: Sacramento

1) Wikipedia; Sac. Buccaneers, Sac Capitals

2) Pro Football Reference; Capitals, Buccaneers

3) The News and Observer; Saturday....October 28, 1967 Raleigh, N.C. Sports in brief page 15

4) Sacramento Bee; Friday...July 25, 1969 (page 58) Sacramento, CA, Photo

5) Sacramento Bee; Sunday... November 30, 1969 Sacramento CA...Cowboys Wallop Caps (page 83)

6) (6)Sacramento Bee; Sunday...July 23, 1989 (pages 39+51) Sacramento, CA Wild and Crazy

7) Sacramento Bee Thursday.... August 10, 1989 Sacramento Bee Game Ad

8) Sacramento Bee; Sunday...August 13, 1989 (page 41) Sacramento, CA Last Minute Touchdown

Chapter Two: WLAF 1991

(1) League Media Guides; 1991 & 1992

(2) Sacramento Media Guides 1991 & 1992

(3) Wikipedia: WLAF 1991 season

(4) Wikipedia: Surge 1991 season

(5) Pro Football Reference; Surge 1991 season

(6) Orangevale News: Wednesday, June 20, 1990 (pages 14-15)
Folsom, CA. WLAF coming to Sacramento

(7) Orlando Sentinel: Saturday, June 6, 1990, (page 19)
Orlando, FLA (other editions), Sacramento is 6th city

(8) Star Tribune: Sunday, November 4, 1990, (page 64)
Minneapolis, MN Team Awarded to Owner

(9) The Press-Tribune: Thursday, November, 15, 1990 (page
10) Roseville, CA. WLAF, Sacramento set for '91

(10) The Dispatch: Tuesday, November 20, 1990, (page 22)
Moline, Ill. Transactions–Football

(11) The Californian: Wednesday, December 5, 1990, (page 17)
Salinas, CA. New Team Named.

(12) Clarion–Ledger: Friday…December 21, 1990 (page 32)
Jackson, Miss 50 Game Schedule Released

(13) Napa Valley Register; Saturday December 22, 1990 (page 12)
Napa Valley,CA Stephenson Named Head Coach

Chapter Three: WLAF 1992

Wikipedia; 1992 WLAF, 1992 Surge, 1992 World Bowl

Media Guides; 1992 Surge, WLAF league guide, 1992 World Bowl

Newspapers.com

Surge box scores all from the Sacramento Bee vs
Montreal…………..Sunday March 15,1992 page 82 (pre-season) vs
Birmingham…….Sunday   March   22,1992   page   46   vs

Ohio................Monday March 30,1992 page 50 vs Montreal........... Sunday April 5,1992 page 84 vs San Antonio......Sunday April 12,1992 page 78 vs Birmingham......Sunday April 19,1992 page 66 vs London............Monday April 27,1992 page 48 vs Montreal..........Monday May 4,1992 page 52 vs Frankfurt........ Sunday May 10,1992 page 48 vs Ohio...............Sunday May 17,1992 page 56 vs San Antonio....Sunday May 24,1992 page 58 vs Barcelona......Monday June 1,1992 page 47 (playoff) vs Orlando.........Sunday June 7,1992 page 44 (World Bowl)

Chapter Four: Arena League 1992

Arena League Record Book 2013

Arena Football media guide 1992

Arenafan.com Sacramento Attack team history 1992

Wikipedia.....Arena Football League 1992 Season

Sacramento Attack 1992 season

Denver Dynamite 1991 season

Pro Football Archives..... Joe Kapp

Sacramento Attack 1992

Newspapers. Com

* Los Angeles Times ; March 6,1992 page 325

Kapp to coach new L.A. team.....Los Angeles,CA

* Intelligencer Journal; March 6,1992 page 23

League announces L.A. team ……Lancaster,PA

* Charlotte Observer; March 26,1992 page 23

Charlotte Rage schedule with L.A. Wings on it

Charlotte, N.C.

* Los Angeles Times; April 6,1992 page 656

Attack name is a natural Los Angeles, CA

* Detroit Free Press; July 17,1992 page 152

Ticket misprint…….Detroit,Mich

* Sacramento Bee: June 12,1992 page 35

Game Ad………. Sacramento,CA

* San Francisco Examiner: July 12,1991 page 76

Wings Bike Team…..San Francisco,CA

* Orangevale News; May 13, 1992 page 17

Operated by Kings owner…..Folsom, CA

Attack box scores (all but one are from the Sacramento Bee Newspaper)

   (1) Saturday; May 30,1992 …… page 56

   (2) Friday; June 5,1992………page 38

   (3) Sunday; June 14,1992……..page 48 (The Arizona Republic)

   (4) Sunday; June 21,1992…….page 48

   (5) Saturday; June 27,1992….page 60

   (6) Tuesday ; July 7,1992……page 50

   (7) Saturday; July 11, 1992…page 34

(8) Saturday; July 18,1992….page 56

(9) Friday; July 24,1992….page 40

(10) Friday; July 31,1992…page 80

(11) Saturday; August 8,1992 …Page 38

Chapter Five: CFL '92–'93

Wikipedia…..1991 NFL season

Remember the PSFL.com

Wikipedia….PSFL 1992

Arena Football League 1992 media guide

Wikipedia…1992 WLAF season

Ottawa Senators..1992 media guide

1992 CFL Record Book

Rochester Rockets…..WNY Heritage…Summer 2022 pages 28–37

The Rise and Fall of the Rochester Rockets Rochester Democrat and Chronicle….page 31…September 4,1956

New York Bid….November 30,1992….The Gazette..page 55

Montreal,Que…Canada…Top Player Flutie

Halifax Bid…November 4,1982….page 35

Johnson City Press-Chronicle…..Johnson City,Tenn

The Star…….October 28,1983…..page 34

Whitehorse,Yukon…Canada

USFL/CFL …Tampa Bay Tribune….page 33

Tampa Bay, FL…….. November 11,1986

Tampa Bay Times….other editions(not main edition)

XFL/CFL ….CBS sports.com….March 10,2021

CBS Sports.com….March 10,2021…

USA Today.com…..July 7,2021….Chris Bumbaca

Larry Smith….1992 CFL record book

Larry Smith….Wikipedia. com

Portland game….Pro Football Archives….1992 CFL season

Calgary against Toronto….Portland, OR.

WLAF on hold…..Sacramento Bee…..December 4,1992…page 36

Sacramento ,Calif. …….The Next Step

4 teams to CFL ……The Leader Post…..November 12,1992

Regina, Saskatchewan, Canada…..page 29

January 19,1993…..page 43

Sac/S.A. added… The Odessa American…January 15,1993

Story with logos……page 25

Miami Game……March 12,1996…Page 81

The Palm Beach Post…..West Palm Beach, Fla.

Pro Football Archives; 1995 Baltimore Stallions

SAN ANTONIO….. brief history

Wikipedia: WLAF 1991…..1992 Season

San Antonio Riders history

San Antonio Force history

Newspapers.com…..Austin American–Statesman….page 57

San Antonio lands CFL team….January 13,1992

Victoria Advocate…..January 29,1993….page 13

San Antonio CFL team put on hold until 1994

Chapter Six: CFL 1993 (part one)

1993 CFL Record Book and Manuel

1994 CFL Record Book and Manuel

1993 Sacramento Gold Miners Media Guide

1994 Sacramento Gold Miners Media Guide

Wikipedia 1993 CFL season

1993 Sacramento Gold Miners season

1994 CFL season

1994 Sacramento Gold Miners season

Chapter Seven: CFL 1993 (part two)

1993 CFL Record Book and Manuel

1994 CFL Record Book and Manuel

Wikipedia 1993 CFL season

1994 CFL season

1993 Sacramento Gold Miners season

1994 Sacramento Gold Miners season

Sacramento Gold Miners media guides; 1993, 1994

Chapter Eight: CFL '94–'95

Wikipedia; CFL season….1994, 1995

Sacramento Gold Miners… 1994 season

San Antonio Texans ….1995 season

CFL Record Book and Manuel…..1994, 1995, 1996

Pro Football Archives…1994, 1995 CFL seasons

Chapter Nine: In Conclusion

Wikipedia; United Football League…2009, 2010, 2011, 2012

Sacramento Mountain Lions…..2010, 2011, 2012 seasons

Pro Football Archives….Sacramento Mountain Lions
2010, 2011, 2012 seasons

About the Author

Gary's love of football started at a young age after watching his first Buffalo Bills game. He would read, watch and collect anything related to the sport. He would study facts about all leagues. Four years ago, Gary started to write about the sport and writes for two magazines on a regular basis. It was this love that helped him to discover the facts found in this book. He also founded the Buffalo Destroyers Museum of the Arena Football League.

Acknowledgments

I would like to thank Greg T. for his support and aid in making this book happen. Jake S. for his help with this story.

I would like to thank my savior, Jesus, as well.

You can view pictures that support this book on my Facebook page.